Circle of the Sun

Rites and Celebrations for Egyptian Pagans and Kemetics

Sharon LaBorde

Circle of the Sun: Rites and Celebrations for Egyptian Pagans and Kemetics.

ISBN: 978-1-105-49837-4

Acknowledgements

This book would not be what it is without the input and support of some very special people. Many heartfelt thanks go to the members of the *Following the Sun* forum, for your concerns, questions and disagreements - all of those have made my writing better and insights broader. Thanks also to Krys Garnett for all those photos from Egypt; to my "repeat offender" Nic M. for his input on correspondences; and most especially, unequivocally, to my husband Daryn - for all the late nights, joys and frustrations. Your love and patience cannot be rewarded enough.

To Dad,
who flew West with the New Moon, April 2011,
with love

Circle of the Sun
Rites and Celebrations for Egyptian Pagans and Kemetics

Table of Contents

Introduction

A few years ago, the Dallas-Fort Worth airport decided to promote the touring "Tutankhamun and the Golden Age of the Pharaohs" exhibit by placing a twenty-six-foot statue of Anubis in the middle of Founders Plaza. *The Dallas Morning News* covered the event in an online article, describing Anubis as "that wacky Egyptian god with the head of a jackal and the body of a human." The author probably had no idea what kind of backlash his description would unleash. It's not as if anyone still worships Anubis anymore, right?

"Your comments about the god Anubis are very offensive," chastised one commenter.

"I hope...the great god Anubis forgives those who disrespected him," warned another.

Skeptical, another reader expressed doubts that there was *really* anyone still "practicing the religion of the pharoh's [*sic*]".

When someone else responded that they indeed did, the skeptic responded, "you may be 'it' " - only to be informed by further posters that the first one was indeed *not* "it", as they too worshipped Egyptian or even Greek and Egyptian gods, and they knew others who did the same. The brief cyber-war ended not long thereafter, but an enlightening point had been made.

Yes, there *are* people today who worship the Egyptian gods. More people, in fact, than most of their peers might think.

Indeed, increasing numbers of people are taking up the worship of Egyptian gods and goddesses. Today there are at least sixteen different legally incorporated groups practicing some form of Egyptian Paganism, also called *Kemetic* religion or Kemeticism. Some of these groups are fairly well-known in the greater Pagan community and have a strong online presence. Others are more obscure and "unplugged", relying mostly upon face-to-face interaction. Some groups are stridently Afrocentric; others are open to all ethnicities.

But Egyptian Paganism-Kemeticism stretches beyond one single group or tradition. It constitutes an entire religious *movement*, one that traces its modern roots back more than a century and now claims adherents across the globe. It has varying sects and traditions, and one could even argue, fundamentalists. Increasingly, Egyptian Paganism counts another population as well: Solitaries, or as they often call themselves, "Independent Kemetics". These independent practitioners are truly the underside of the proverbial iceberg - impossible to count and, unlike the iceberg, growing in number with each passing year.

But despite this burgeoning online presence of Egyptian Paganism-Kemeticism; the growing number of Egyptian Pagans attending Pagan festivals every year, as well as books published about various sects of the religion; and even lawsuits involving members of Kemetic groups, the movement still finds itself frequently snubbed by other Pagans. For example, in her 1993 book To Ride a Silver Broomstick, Silver Ravenwolf listed a host of different traditions of Wicca, including Gardnerian, Alexandrian, Dianic and Eclectic. But she failed to mention Tameran Wicca, which adapts Egyptian religion to Wiccan practice. Nor did she mention the Reconstructionist (i.e. Kemetic) form, even in a context of general Pagan Reconstructionism. In another example coming nearly two decades later, Thea Sabin's 2011 Wicca for Beginners still neglected to mention Tameran Wicca in its overview of traditions; yet many of the young Wiccans emerging from what the author dubbed "Generation Hex" are specifically asking questions about Tameran Wicca and the worship of Egyptian deities.

More confusingly, as those newcomers to Egyptian Paganism continue to explore their options and learn about other sects besides Tameran Wicca, they encounter a bewildering number of distinctions. What should they consider themselves - Tameran Wiccan or Kemetic? If they decide upon Kemetic, what kind are they - Still Wiccan? Or Eclectic? Reconstructionist? 'Orthodox'? Worse, will their own ethnicity count against them if they look for Kemetic groups online?

Indeed, while Egyptian Paganism constitutes the singular, shared desire of people around the world to revive the worship of ancient Egyptian deities, its multiplicity of viewpoints are often addressed to the exclusion of one another.

The rituals, rites and background information in the pages to come are meant to offer a useful starting ground for all Egyptian Pagans. Whether you count yourself as a Tameran Wiccan, honoring a pair such as Osiris and Isis as the Lord and Lady; a Kemetic Reconstructionist looking for rites based on ancient texts for your personal practice; an Isian Pagan looking for material to incorporate into your own tradition; or a more eclectic Pagan seeking to honor an Egyptian god or goddess in your own way, you are invited to seek inspiration here. For those interested in coming together to build their own Tameran or Kemetic traditions and groups, the final chapter offers helpful topics to consider as well as information on Egyptian priesthoods and ideas for group initiations. Others who prefer to remain Independent can find information on self-initiation, choosing a religious name and other topics. In either case, the knowledge offered is meant to empower more Egyptian Pagans and Kemetics to continue following and building upon their faith well into the Twenty-First century - more people just like you.

So, *Iiu em hotep* ("Welcome")!

Our Place in History

Modern Pagans are often keenly aware of the end of original pagan worship, and thus the subsequent gap between their spiritual forbears and themselves. Egyptian Pagans are no different. Privately and across Internet forums, the question often comes up: when did ancient people stop worshiping the Egyptian gods? We know that ancient Egyptian religion was finally supplanted by Christianity, but how long ago, and under what circumstances? Where did we "leave off", so to speak?

To this question we will add another, equally important one: when did people *start* worshiping them *again*? Because to understand our own place in the history of humankind's search for the Divine, we must answer both. The Egyptian Pagan movement can only be greater served by understanding its own history, and thus its relationship to present social, academic, and greater Neo-Pagan trends.

In the Not-Too-Distant Past

Many people take as a given that the polytheistic religions of Egypt, Greece and Rome died quickly as Christianity spread throughout the Mediterranean during the first and second centuries C.E. Scholars of Late Antiquity in particular view the people of that period as somehow 'destined' to embrace Christianity because paganism supposedly no longer met their needs. The official conversion point is considered to be Emperor Theodosius' edicts of 380 and 381 C.E., which outlawed pagan temples and established Nicene Christianity as the state religion. But in the case of Egypt, the old gods did not become demoted to mere ghost stories until the Muslim conquest some three centuries later. Thus the "gap" between the end of original pagan Egyptian worship somewhere during the 600's C.E. and the beginning of Pagan (or Neo-Pagan) revival in the 1900's C.E. is a relatively short thirteen centuries. When we explore the last millennium of pagan Egypt, we discover that it actually has quite a few commonalities with our modern renaissance of Egyptian Paganism. The more we examine that era's final chapter, the more we can appreciate the beginning of our own.

Innovation Through Adversity: The Third Intermediate and Late Periods

It would be wrong to assume that the last phase of "true" Egyptian religion ended with the Ramesside pharaohs. The idea of a strong king was central to Egyptians' view of an ordered cosmos; but when rulership of the country fragmented into power struggles and civil war during the Third Intermediate Period (approx. 1080-747 B.C.E.), average Egyptians certainly did not stop practicing their religion for want of a pharaoh. They simply adapted with the changing times, giving new meanings to traditional ideas.

The city of Thebes had not served as the capital of Egypt since Rameses II had moved his administration to the Delta during the late New Kingdom. A century later, the capital shifted with changing political fortunes to the northern city of Tanis, then to Bubastis. The clergy of Thebes actually revolted against King Takelot II, who ruled from Tanis. His son, Prince Osorkon, travelled to Thebes and had all of the priests who rebelled executed. The failed rebellion is recorded in the so-called Bubastite Portal in Karnak temple. Four years later, Thebes revolted again, and it was another decade before peace was finally made!

This chaotic and decentralized civil order had an effect upon average Egyptians' artistic and religious expressions. Wealthy Egyptians ceased commissioning large decorated tombs, probably because they must have felt that such expensive projects had no guarantee of protection by civil authorities. However, smaller arts burgeoned during this time period, and the themes used in these works of art, such as stelae (round-topped tablets) and sculptures, continued certain important trends. For example, toward the end of the New Kingdom private tomb art had begun to show citizens adoring their gods directly in the Underworld, *Duat*. Before that time, adoration of the gods was considered a royal prerogative; citizens depicted themselves receiving offerings from descendants or enjoying eternal life in *Duat*. By the Third Intermediate and Late Periods, commissioning a stela for one's burial or for memorial in a temple was a safer investment than a frescoed tomb chapel, but the images on those stelae were almost exclusively of individuals worshiping the gods in person. Increasingly, the people pictured adoring the gods were women. Before, a husband would usually commission tomb art or a memorial stela for the whole family. By the Late Period, more individuals were buying religious goods for themselves. The art they bought placed less emphasis on the family as subjects of the king, and more upon the person as a follower of the gods.

Bronze casting reached its height in the Late Period, which meant that small bronze statues could be purchased much more easily. Scores of these votives, in the form of popular deities such as Bast, Sakhmet, Isis, Ptah and others, were placed by individuals into various temples. Often the statuettes contained dedicatory inscriptions relating who had bought them, so that the gods would favor them. Like the personal stelae, these votive statues reflected a greater concern for personal intercession.

The roles that many deities filled for their worshipers also changed. In times past, Osiris and Isis were mostly revered in a funerary context, either when someone died or during festivals for the dead. But into the Late Period, Osiris also came to be regarded as lord of the living. Multiple chapels to Osiris were built in the temple of Amun at Thebes, where his name was written in cartouches like a king's with titles such as "Lord of Life" and "Ruler of Eternity". Isis, once the prototypical widow and mother of the reigning king, became an ideal universal mother as her popularity surged. In turn, Horus' aspect as a child, Hor-pa-khered, took on increasing importance. Together with Isis, they were invoked for the protection of mothers and children. A new type of stone statue, called a *cippus* (plural *cippi*,) featured Horus the Child standing naked on top of crocodiles and holding other dangerous animals in his hands. Spells and stories of Isis curing Horus of stings or snakebite were inscribed all over the front, back and sides. Water would be poured over the *cippus* and then drunk by someone afflicted by bites, stings or other ailments in an effort to partake of Hor-pa-khered's healing powers.

Ra and Osiris became increasingly linked, with Osiris taking on solar associations - being hailed in hymns as reborn with the morning sun, for example - and Ra descending into the Underworld to reunite with his body as Osiris. Themes of the sun god's nocturnal journey through *Duat*, once a privilege of kings, now appeared on the coffins of nonroyal citizens. Just as instability during the First Intermediate Period had the effect of "opening up" the royal liturgy of the Pyramid Texts to the (paying) masses, so too did the breakdown of dynasties in the Third Intermediate Period allow further dissemination of once-guarded religious motifs. The sun bark of Ra took on a far greater capacity, as ordinary Egyptians and not just pharaohs hoped to find passage on it through the Underworld!

Osiris, Isis, Horus the Child and Ra in his falcon-headed form are so familiar to us today because they reached a peak in popularity in their homeland during a critical point: Alexander the Great's conquest of Persia, which made Greece the dominant empire and Egypt one of its territories. As part of this new Hellenistic world, Egypt's well-evolved religious fabric would begin to interweave with that of Western culture's beginnings.

Egypt Under the Ptolemies

Alexander might have been welcomed by the Egyptians as a savior who delivered their country from the Persians, but his general Ptolemy and the dynasty he founded in Egypt did not completely reciprocate the people's enthusiasm. The Ptolemies kept their Greek language and culture, which became the preferred language of trade, and their political interests were often turned toward other Greek holdings. Ptolemy IV fought a war against Antiochos III, who ruled the Seleucid Empire, stretching from modern-day Syria and Turkey to what is now Pakistan. Ptolemy IV won, but the Egyptian soldiers who fought for him evidently became emboldened enough to consider life without a Greek overlord. Thereafter began the most frequently-overlooked period in Egyptian history: the revolt against the Ptolemies.

The revolt began in the southern city of Edfu. A year or two later, in 205 B.C.E., the first native king in over a hundred years was crowned in Thebes: Hor-onnefer (Haronnophris). He launched a guerrilla war against the Ptolemies, attacking the temples because they benefitted from the Ptolemies and served as major engines of commerce. Hor-onnefer was killed, but his successor Ankh-Onnofer (Chaonnophris) was crowned in 199 B.C.E. and fought for another five years before meeting his own end. But their revolt had spread through much of the country, even into the Delta near Alexandria, and delayed construction of the famous temple of Edfu. Inscriptions in Edfu refer to the rebellion, and references to Ptolemy V's victory over rebels outside Alexandria come from none other than the Rosetta Stone. Revolts still continued to break out periodically. Records survive of one begun by a Petosiris in 164 B.C.E., by Harseisis in 130 B.C.E., and finally a general revolt in Thebes in 88 B.C.E. that caused substantial damage to the city.

The named leaders of these rebellions share a significant common theme. They all derived their names from appellations of either Horus or Osiris, whose traditional title was "Unnefer", or "the Beatified". Recall that Osiris had become much more than just lord of the Underworld; he was the divine ruler of justice, whose son Horus had became a savior who championed his father and set the world aright. The Ptolemies tried to co-opt this theme using the traditional festival of Horus at Edfu, presenting themselves as the true avatars of Horus. Not all of the native Egyptians accepted this presentation, as witnessed by the multiple attempts at revolution by people bearing Horus' name. We may never know whether the general population became divided over support for the foreign-born Ptolemies versus nationalism, but social unrest seemed to continue. Crowd control at local festivals became a greater and greater issue for the Ptolemies, and processions became more and more restricted.

The Ptolemies also faced domestic unrest, as successive members of the family vied with one another for claim to the throne. Increasingly, they turned to the emerging Rome to arbitrate their disputes. Ptolemy Auletes (XII) essentially bribed the Romans to recognize his rule, which made him so unpopular in Alexandria that Roman garrisons became necessary to keep the peace! When he died in 51 B.C.E., his will specified that his daughter, Cleopatra VII, and his son Ptolemy XIII would rule jointly under Rome's guardianship. This co-regency quickly degenerated, with Cleopatra seeking the aid of Julius Caesar...and we know what eventually happened.

For most Egyptians, life under the Romans continued much as it had under the Ptolemies. Roman emperors presented themselves as pharaohs in the occasional temple dedication. Literate Egyptians were frequently bilingual or even trilingual, speaking Egyptian, Greek, and sometimes Nubian or Aramaic, in order to ply their trades in an increasingly cosmopolitan society. Greeks and Romans who came to Egypt often adopted Egyptian customs and worship, but gave it a Hellenic twist. Generally the Egyptians resisted assimilating Greek or Roman culture, regarding it as 'unclean' and 'foreign'. Much has already been written about Isis' spread throughout the Mediterranean world. The new Isis religion, which combined Egyptian elements with Hellenistic mystery religions, offered followers direct intercession and personal salvation, themes which traced back to Isis' native ascendancy in the Late Period. But the Isis religion soon found a powerful competitor from the region of Judea.

End of an Era: The Romans and Copts

By the second or third century A.D., the majority of the famous temples associated with Egypt's pharaonic era - Karnak, Thebes, Memphis and Heliopolis - were in an advanced state of decline. But smaller temples and local shrines built by citizens continued to function, the latter being officiated at during feast days by rotating clergy. By this time many local deities had absorbed into Isis, Serapis (Hellenized Osiris) and a handful of other major gods such as Sobek. By way of example, Isis' identification with the Greek earth goddess Demeter abroad may have come from her local absorption of Rennutet, the cobra goddess of nourishment and good harvests.

Temples gradually lost funding and support from their Roman overlords, eventually being shut down completely. Meanwhile, pagan Egyptian practices became more localized. Some wealthy patrons maintained icons in their own estates, hosting feast days for their towns at their own expense. One such patron was Gesios of Panopolis (Akhmim, traditional home of the god Min). Whether he intended to or not, Gesios became something of an arch-rival to the Coptic Christian bishop Shenoute, who used his sermons to paint Gesios as a "rich pagan" who oppressed the local Christian converts. Shenoute railed against folk practices such as lighting terra-cotta lamps at feast days and offering incense to household icons, branding the gods represented as 'demons' and people venerating them as 'sinners'. Meanwhile, Shenoute's mobs broke into Gesios' estate to steal the 'idols' within and vandalize their shrines. Shenoute was eventually arrested and tried in the town of Antinoopolis for stealing sacred scrolls and destroying the temple in nearby Plewit, as well as vandalizing Gesios' shrines in Panopolis.

The destruction of the Serapeum in Alexandria by a Christian mob in 391 A.D. is sometimes cited as heralding the end of Egyptian religion. However, the ideological war waged by Shenoute and his followers against Gesios of Panopolis took place in the following century. Other documents show that Nubians living near Philae, in the south of Egypt, still made regular pilgrimages to the temple in order to take an icon of Isis in procession well into the Sixth century. In still more cases, Christian evangelism only served to give a different "flavor" to older folk practices that they could not supplant; such as the use of amulets and magic (*heka*) and consulting oracles, now in the form of holy men. Sites considered sacred by pagan forebears, such as the temples of Luxor and Deir el-Bahari, were still esteemed enough by Coptic Christians for them to build a church in Luxor and a monastery in Deir el-Bahari! Later still, Muslim Egyptians built a mosque amidst Luxor temple, part of which still stands today.

Coptic Christianity continued in Egypt, though it found itself the minority religion following the Arab conquest of 639-641 C.E. Islam more thoroughly displaced pagan beliefs and practices than the Coptic Church had, but echoes persisted. The most famous example is the Abu al-Haggag festival in Thebes, which even today honors a Muslim saint but takes place during the same time of year as the ancient Festival of the Valley. A small boat loaded onto a cart is paraded through town, though *sans* icons of Amun or Mut. Villagers no longer hold picnics at the graves of their loved ones, but instead bring food to the cemeteries where local poor and homeless wait to receive them. The old religious elements have long gone, but the activities associated with them have taken on new meanings within the framework of Islam.

A Re-Awakening Begins

Naturally, the old religion of Egypt could not revive instantly from so long a slumber as thirteen centuries. But its first tenuous breaths of new life came surprisingly early, and in unexpected places.

Well-read Europeans of the post-Renaissance era might have been aware of Isis and Osiris from Plutarch's description in his multi-part work *Moralia*. But in 1749, the ancient Roman town of Pompeii was discovered, having been preserved and buried under volcanic debris. After a few years of initial excavation, Pompeii's Temple of Isis was uncovered, almost completely intact. The town quickly became something of a tourist attraction, and in 1769 the thirteen-year-old musical prodigy Mozart visited it. His sightseeing at the Temple of Isis is thought to have inspired him twenty years later when he co-wrote *The Magic Flute*, an opera that includes major singing parts by actors playing priests of Isis and Osiris! *The Magic Flute* also had major Masonic themes, as both Mozart and co-author Emanuel Schikander were Freemasons. Masonic societies would eventually come to play a major role in the evolution of Egyptian-themed occultism.

Interest in ancient Egyptian lore found fertile ground on both sides of the Atlantic. In America, the Spiritualist Movement that began in the mid-19th century created widespread interest in mankind's "spiritual evolution". The often eclectic beliefs found in Spiritualism gave rise to new religious groups that were precursors to what we know today as the "New Age" movement. One of these groups, the Theosophical Society, was founded in New York in 1875. Theosophy co-founder Madame Blavatsky wrote Isis Unveiled in 1877; the two-volume work criticized inconsistencies in Judeo-Christianity, comparing many of its tenets with those of Qabalah, Eastern religions and ancient Egyptian mythology. Theosophy's motto stated, "There is no religion higher than truth," and it posited that all modern religions draw from, often distorting, ancient original truths. Following Madame Blavatsky's death, Theosophy split into several groups, one of which would relocate to Pasadena, California.

Another group to receive influence from Theosophy was an offshoot of Freemasonry, the Hermetic Order of the Golden Dawn. Their first temple, Isis-Urania, was founded in London in 1888. Later temples founded elsewhere in Britain were named Osiris, Horus and Amen-Ra. Combining ceremonial magic, Qabalah mysticism and other sources with ancient Egyptian elements, the Hermetic Order became extremely popular, and among its members were English poet William Butler Yeats and a certain Aleister Crowley.

Into the Twentieth Century

Crowley is already well known among historians of both modern Paganism and ceremonial magic. He created his own system, Thelema, based on revelations he claimed to receive from the god

Horus while visiting Cairo, Egypt in 1904. Thelema drew extensively from Egyptian religion (although using translations of names now proven to be faulty), again combining them with eclectic elements. Late in his life, Crowley befriended Gerald Gardner, founder of Wicca. Many of Gardnerian Wicca's rites draw heavily from Crowley's writing.

In 1921 another future influence of Wicca, The Witch-Cult in Western Europe, was published by Margaret Murray. Dr. Murray was an Egyptologist working at the Manchester Museum in London, where she had led a groundbreaking interdisciplinary project to unwrap and study two mummies. Anthropology was her secondary pursuit, and unfortunately her scholarship in Witch-Cult, as well as its follow-up books The God of the Witches in 1933 and The Divine King in England in 1954, was proven to be highly questionable. But despite these works being dismissed as "vapid balderdash", in the words of one academic critic, they were eagerly accepted by Gerald Gardner and other founding members of what was to become Wicca. She even wrote the foreword to Gardner's 1951 book, Witchcraft Today.

Pagan Reconstructionism, defined as modern Pagan religions that attempt to recreate ancient prototypes such as Greek or Egyptian religion, is generally thought of as a recent phenomenon. But the first Pagan Reconstructionist church was actually founded in 1938. The Long Island Church of Aphrodite was begun by a Russian immigrant, Gleb Botkin, who wrote liturgy and rites for the worship of Aphrodite, whom he viewed as the sole Goddess of creation. It did not long outlive its founder, but the Church of Aphrodite represents the first Pagan Reconstructionist group in America.

At the same time that Gardner was developing Wiccan rites with his coven in England in the 1950's, a group of high school friends in California started their own countercultural club called the "Chesley Donovan Science Fantasy Foundation". One of its founding members, Harold Moss, was a native of Pasadena whose parents were Theosophists. After watching *The Egyptian* in 1954, Moss and his friends in Chesley Donovan adopted the pharaoh Akhenaton as their mascot and began wearing ankhs. Eventually they came to admire all of Egyptian religion, and in 1964 they began a tradition of hosting Egyptian costume parties, which eventually were scheduled to coincide with the traditional Egyptian New Year in mid-July. Moss also began to meet people in the growing Pagan community, and with the help of his Chesley Donovan and newfound Pagan friends, the Church of the Eternal Source was founded on August 30, 1970. It was legally incorporated the following year. The first Egyptian Reconstructionist group was born.

The Church of the Eternal Source disagrees with the use of the word "Kemetic", and in fact they predate the term by probably three years. In 1973 R. A. Straughn, an African-American member of the Rosicrucian Anthropological League, founded his own tradition called the Ausar-Auset Society. Rosicrucianism, a society related to the Hermetic Order of the Golden Dawn, claimed to be descended from Eighteenth-Dynasty Egyptian priests. It was a segregated society, however, and the Rosicrucian Anthropological League was the branch designated for African-Americans. R. A. Straughn, now calling himself Ra Un Nefer Amen, incorporated elements of Hermeticism such as the Tree of Life into a more specifically Egyptian framework for the Ausar-Auset Society. An Afrocentric organization, the Ausar-Auset Society was probably the first group to adopt the word *Kemetic* to refer to Egyptian religion from a 'native', more specifically African, perspective.

The mid-1970's saw even more firsts in modern Egyptian Paganism. The first Isian Wiccan coven, the Star of the Gold Cross coven, was founded by Margot Dana in 1974; one year later, Temple Harakhte was begun, drawing influence from the writings of Omm Seti (born Dorothy Eady), a British woman who claimed to have been a priestess of Isis in a past life; and in 1976 the Fellowship of Isis was founded by Olivia Robertson in Ireland. By this point, all of the major branches of Egyptian Paganism had been established: Egyptian/Kemetic Reconstructionist, Isian, Tameran Wiccan, and a host of eclectic Egyptian groups in between.

Another factor critical to the development of Kemetic Reconstructionism made major advancements in the 1970's and 80's: specifically, the non-specialist publication of newer English translations of major ancient Egyptian texts. The Pyramid Texts, Coffin Texts and Book of the Dead were all translated by Raymond O. Faulkner and published in book form between 1969 and 1985. Miriam Lichtheim's three-volume work, Ancient Egyptian Literature, was released from 1973 to 1980; and a host of other Egyptology books, such as Herman te Velde's Seth, God of Confusion and Rosalie David's A Guide to Religious Ritual at Abydos, also saw print during this timeframe. These works, now accessible to the greater public and not just the academic community, would become primary sources of background information and liturgy for Egyptian and Kemetic groups.

Reputedly following a vision of the goddess Sakhmet received during a ritual, in 1988 Wiccan priestess Tamara Siuda founded Per Bast with a handful of fellow Chicago-area Pagans. In 1993 this group would be reformed and incorporated as the House of Netjer, or Kemetic Orthodoxy. The House of Netjer quickly found a following among users of the nascent Internet by using live IRC chats and online forums to facilitate communication between members spanning various continents.

That same year outside Las Vegas, Nevada, philanthropist and activist Genevieve Vaughan finally fulfilled a promise she had made to Sakhmet following the birth of her daughters by constructing an open-air Temple of Sakhmet. Echoing the role that Isis once held for Greco-Roman devotees as the "Goddess of 10,000 Names", in the Nevada temple Sakhmet continues to be honored as the Universal Goddess and is officiated by a resident priestess.

A New Millennium

As the 1990's wore on, controversy seemed to brew within the House of Netjer, in particular over Siuda's role as the "*nisut*", or pharaoh (a word eschewed by members) of the organization. Supporters felt having a pharaonic figure necessary to represent the spirit of Horus incarnate among humankind; but dissenters felt it placed too much central authority and control into one person. Various offshoot groups eventually incorporated, including Akhet Hwt-Hrw in 1998 and Per Ankh in 2000. In 2001 another, much more obscure Egyptian group, Nuhati am Nutjeru, incorporated with its own *nisut* as the group leader. In a sense, modern Egyptian Paganism has come full circle to its Late Period antecedent: an increasingly introspective faith actively pursued by individual followers, but with multiple figureheads each laying claim the divine throne of Horus.

And just as Isis, Osiris, Horus and Ra-Horakhety held immense popularity in the last centuries of original Egyptian religion, today They continue to draw in new followers along with Bast and Anubis - two other favorite deities of Late Antiquity who are extremely popular today- as well as Sakhmet and others. Some modern adherents seek initiation into present-day descendants of the Greco-Roman mystery religions, just as millions who worshipped Isis in the ancient world became Her initiates. Other modern Pagans prefer something that more closely resembles native Egyptian practices, taking up a Reconstructionist path instead. Together, all of these facets of current Egyptian Paganism mirror the eclectic religious landscape of Egypt some fourteen centuries ago, while at the same time taking the Egyptian gods into directions that could never have been imagined in ancient times. The past has always been among Egyptian faith's greatest inspirations in forging new paths toward the future. Now, both distant and recent past continue to be our allies as we forge ahead.

Kemetic Theology

Is there a God? A Goddess? Many Gods?
If so, what is He or She, or what are They, like?
If the God, Goddess, or Gods are all-powerful,
then why is there suffering in the world?

If you've ever asked yourself any of these questions, or talked about them among your friends or family, congratulations: you've discussed theology.

Usually the word *theology* is associated with Christianity, but as *theos*, "god", *logia*, "study", it can be applied to the study of the Divine in virtually any religion. To put it another way, theology represents a given religion's way of explaining itself and how it views its 'Higher Powers'. While Tameran practice largely follows the established patterns of Wicca, as we will explore below, it looks to the same source of inspiration as Kemetic Reconstructionism; so for the purpose of exploring their shared theology, the two branches of Egyptian Paganism will be covered inclusively in this section. The ancient Egyptian view of the world and the Divine has given both modern traditions certain unique perspectives that form the cornerstones of Kemetic theology. So what are they?

Non-exclusivity: Kemetic belief does not at any point claim to hold "the" absolutely correct answer (group ideologies notwithstanding), nor are its gods the "only" ones. This inclusiveness is actually a hallmark of polytheistic faiths, both ancient and modern;

it stands in contrast to the monotheistic view that only one deity, one possibility, exists in the Universe.

Non-exclusivity is particularly necessary in Egyptian religion because it claims multiple creation stories. Who first fashioned the world? Was it Ra? Ptah? Neith? Whereas most modern Western thought looks for an "either-or" answer, Kemetic theology posits a different one entirely: "all of them". Egyptologist Erik Hornung compared Egyptian multiplicity of viewpoints to the modern science of quantum physics. To give a simple example, the question "Is light a particle or a wave?" had in the past vexed physicists because light has properties of both particles *and* waves. An exclusive, 'either-or' approach cannot explain the problem. Quantum physics, particularly in "many-worlds interpretation", has had to adopt what is actually a traditional Egyptian approach: all answers are valid, often simultaneously, because one answer is not enough to describe reality.

Cyclical versus linear time: In a similar vein, Kemetic theology views two different forms of time. The first, being linear, is the kind with which we are most familiar today. The ancient Egyptian word *djet*, most commonly translated as "eternity", actually relates to linear time. *Djet* represents time that is eternally continuing forward, what some modern scholars translate as "enduring" time or "eternal sameness".

By contrast, the Egyptian word *neheh*, also traditionally translated as "eternity", in fact refers to time that repeats itself. Newer renderings of *neheh* include "repeating" and "eternally renewing". This cyclical form of time is best exemplified by the movement of the sun; each sunrise is naturally a repeat of the one before, going all the way back to the beginning of the sun and the earth themselves. Egyptians explained this as being a re-living of that first moment of Creation, *Zep Tepi*; it wasn't something that just happened once, long ago, but rather something that continues to happen every morning in cyclical time.

This concept is actually critical for understanding both the Egyptian concept of immortality and certain aspects of deities. In *neheh* time, death is necessary for eternal life because it forms a link in the repeating cycle of renewal. Ra, described as 'Lord of *Neheh*', cyclical time, dies every sunset and is reborn every morning. In this manner, He lives eternally, because He will always be reborn anew. In counterpoint, Osiris is often called 'Lord of *Djet*' as well as *Neheh*, because He both lives in eternal stasis as Ruler of the Underworld and undergoes resurrection each night through His union with Ra.

(Some Kemetics contend that Ra does not actually die when He enters the Underworld; this could be considered a doctrinal difference, but in either interpretation, the principle of cyclical time still applies to Ra's nightly journey.)

Multiple vessels: If more than one deity can play the role of Creator, and can do so repeatedly or even simultaneously, then it follows that a deity can also inhabit more than one "body" or vessel. Spirits of the dead, especially those whom in Egyptian thought have become transfigured or "made *akh*", can also occupy either their preserved physical body or another vessel that has been consecrated to them. The means of consecration and use of icons for deities varies by Kemetic sect, but the underlying principle remains the same. Monotheistic thought generally fails to grasp the concept of a "vessel" for a deity, hence most monotheists perceive the icon (or "idol") to actually *be* the deity in question. But both Kemetic and Eastern faiths, such as Hinduism, Buddhism and Shinto, understand that a statue is simply one form that a being can inhabit. (Tendai Buddhist schools actually have a complex doctrine explaining the innate Buddha-nature of inanimate objects.) The god or spirit invited to inhabit a particular icon is not limited to that one form.

Immanent, but not transcendent, deities: Some religions imagine the Divine to be remote, inaccessible, or beyond the concerns of Its creation. Voudon is one example of a polytheistic religion that considers its original Creator (Olorun in the Yoruba tradition) to be unapproachable by mortals, hence the need for intercession by the *orisha*. This remoteness is the opposite of "immanence", in which deities are present in the world and accessible to the individual. In a related concept, Judeo-Christianity and Islam describe Yahweh/Allah as transcending the limits of space and time. This is what the term "transcendent" usually means in theology.

Egyptian gods and goddesses, by contrast, are considered immanent in the created world and directly accessible to the average worshiper through any number of forms. While They span vastly beyond human limitations, the Gods do not transcend space and time.

This is due to the Egyptian concept of the Universe: everything that exists does so within the limits of Creation and order (*ma'at*), which rests in turn within the chaotic primordial abyss of Nun. If there were no Creation, there would be no Gods. In fact, a common title shared by Ra, Atum and Amun-Ra is "Lord to the Limit", referring to the limits of the created world.

This idea also suggests a Kemetic answer to one of humankind's most basic questions, why is there suffering in the world? Rather than positing that a single, transcendent deity somehow 'wills' or 'allows' suffering, the Egyptian world view interprets the Gods as having limits. Sometimes bad things happen because, in those fleeting moments, Their reach was not quite far enough; or alternatively, that chaos intruded into order before it could be stopped. Indeed, much of Kemetic Reconstructionist ritual in particular is meant to assist the Gods in maintaining the workings of order, *ma'at*, against chaos. Humanity acts as partners, rather than solely as dependents, of the Gods.

Specific interpretations of particular deities, creation stories or other aspects of Egyptian religion naturally vary from one sect of Kemetic, Tameran or other neo-Egyptian practice to the next. But underpinning all of them are these four basic concepts of non-exclusive thought, cyclical time complimenting linear time, the ability of gods or spirits to inhabit multiple vessels and the immanence of the *Notjeru* (or *Netjeru*), the Egyptian gods, in the world. These ideas mark modern Egyptian Paganism as similar to some current faiths, particularly other polytheistic religions such as Hinduism. These concepts also serve to contrast Egyptian Paganism from other faiths, not just Judeo-Christianity and Islam but even some Neo-Pagan traditions such as Discordianism or the Goddess movement. None of these differences make any one faith more or less valid, of course, but they serve to illustrate the uniqueness and value of each.

What Makes Us Different - And the Same

While sharing a common source, Kemetic Reconstructionism and Tameran Wicca have definite variations in how they interpret Egyptian religion. These differences lie in their respective *doctrines*, in other words their specifically defined and broadly accepted principles; and to a lesser extent in their *dogma*, being their specific articles of faith that cannot be disputed. Interestingly, if you were to pick up any book on Wicca, somewhere in the first chapter of nearly all of them you will read some version of the statement that "Wicca has no doctrine and no dogma." But given the definitions above, Wicca does have its own doctrine and, depending on which coven you talk to, its own levels of dogma. Kemetic Reconstructionism certainly has its share of each, again depending upon tradition. Sects of Egyptian Paganism that fall under the categories of Tameran Wicca and Isianism share much of mainstream Wicca's doctrine. Kemetic doctrine is more unique. What are some of these basic tenets?

Nature of the Divine - Wicca is generally either *duotheistic*, seeing the "Lord" and the "Lady" as two divine entities; or *pluriform monotheistic*, recognizing One divine source with male and female aspects, represented by all the known names of gods and goddesses as archetypes. Some Wiccans view all deities as simply aspects of nature or of the subconscious mind, making them technically *atheist*. Tameran Wiccans and Isians may be duotheistic; pluriform monotheist, viewing the original One as perhaps Isis; or more *polytheistic*, treating gods and goddesses as distinct, multiple entities.

Kemetics generally range from *hard polytheists*, meaning that they regard all deities as distinctly separate entities, to *soft polytheists*, who allow for combining of deities to varying degrees. Some are *henotheistic*, acknowledging a vast pantheon but typically concentrating worship on just one god at a time. An interesting exception to this would be some Afrocentric sects of Kemeticism, which view the different Egyptian deities as aspects of either a Divine whole, or else of nature and humanity.

Ethics - Wiccan ethics are generally based upon the Wiccan Rede, which has some variations but most commonly states, "An' it harm none, do as ye will." One exception would be Gardnerian tradition, which follows the "Charge of the Goddess".

Kemetic ethics are expressed in the idiomatic term *ma'at*, which encompasses "truth", "justice", "righteousness" and "order". Kemetics as well as some Tamerans draw ethical guidance from the famous 42 Negative Confessions, also called the Declarations of Innocence, from Chapter 125 of the Book of the Dead. Other sources of translated Egyptian literature, such as the Instructions of Ptah-hotep,

Ani and Amunenope, are also sometimes used.

While most mainstream Wiccans do not believe in a final judgment of the soul, adherents of Egyptian Paganism - both Tameran and Kemetic - frequently do. Eastern beliefs in karma and reincarnation have also been widely adopted by both mainstream Wiccans and Egyptian Pagans alike.

Liturgical Calendar - A major component of Wiccan observance is the Wheel of the Year, a festival cycle of eight Sabbats determined by a combination of the seasons, solar equinoxes and solstices, and monthly dates on the Gregorian calendar. These eight Sabbats of Samhain, Yule, Imbolc, Ostara, Beltane, Litha, Lammas, and Mabon (with variations on certain Sabbat names) honor themes and stages in the life cycle of the God and Goddess. The Sabbats occur roughly one-and-a-half months apart. Wiccans also observe a lunar calendar of Esbats, which honor the three phases of the Goddess (maiden, mother and crone). Tameran Wiccans often have varying levels of success in incorporating Egyptian themes into the Sabbats; Osiris, Isis and Horus tend to adapt most readily to the annual themes of birth, death and renewal.

Meanwhile, the Kemetic calendar is based upon stellar phenomena, specifically the movements of Sirius; and the ancient Egyptian civil calendar, which was divided into twelve months of thirty days with five 'Intercalary' days. The number of Kemetic holidays observed throughout the year varies depending upon specific group tradition or an individual's patron deities; these observances do not necessarily occur at even intervals, although several take place at the beginning or endings of Egyptian months. All Kemetic holidays honor either a major mythological event, such as the anniversary of Creation at New Year's; or a particular deity, such as Thoth (Djehuty) during the Djehutet Festival.

Places of Worship - Wiccans generally prefer outdoor, natural settings for group worship because in Wiccan belief, nature best reflects the Divine. A common expression used in Wicca expresses this philosophy: "As above, so below". Tameran covens typically follow suit for formal rituals, although individual practice is more commonly performed indoors. In a similar vein, both mainstream and Tameran Wiccans use Quarter Calls to invoke the Four Directions and cast a circle before beginning a Sabbat or Esbat ritual.

Kemetic Reconstructionists tend to prefer permanent, indoor settings for both formal group rituals and private worship. Pre-ritual acts of purification may be used, but Kemetic rites do not cast a circle nor call Quarters. Nature is respected as part of the Gods' domain, but Kemetic belief does not eschew man-made settings.

Membership and Officiation - Mainstream Wicca usually follows a three-level degree system; Isian tradition often adds a fourth level for beginners such as "Neophyte". By the time a Wiccan has attained his or her second degree, he or she is considered a priest or priestess. In covens, the goal of each member is to become a priest, and eventually a high priest(ess). When a coven performs a Sabbat or Esbat observance, depending upon tradition it must be officiated by a high priest and priestess, to represent the God and Goddess respectively. The primary exception would be Dianic Wicca, which focuses on the Goddess exclusively. Tameran Wiccan covens typically follow mainstream Wiccan degree systems and officiation in rituals.

Organized Kemetic groups do not require members to pursue a priest ranking, though they may define other levels of membership. One can remain a "lay member" of most Kemetic groups indefinitely. Formal observances can be officiated by one or multiple clergy, but it is not required to have a 'masculine' and 'feminine' representative to perform rituals. Officiants generally can be of either gender. Some groups do not even feminize titles into "priestess" or "high priestess".

Many discussions of modern Paganism tend to either treat Wicca exclusively, or group the kaleidoscope of Neo-Pagan traditions together under broad generalizations. But as our comparison-and-contrast between Kemetic Reconstructionism and Tameran Wicca has illustrated, distinct and even lively differences can emerge between parallel sects. Within the Egyptian Pagan community this sometimes results in a lack of dialogue; often Kemetic Reconstructionists look upon Tameran practice as too “impure”, due to its influences from mainstream Wicca. Meanwhile, Tameran Wiccans feel turned off by the seemingly “hardline” approach of Kemetic Reconstructionism. Doctrinal differences are a part of human nature and destined to emerge in any religious movement. But hopefully this more inclusive look will promote greater understanding, and eventually greater discussion.

Personal Practice

Pagans who participate in a coven, circle or other group typically also follow their own private practices. But for Solitaries and Independent Kemetics, personal practice can represent the whole of their religious activity. Unfortunately, most books written for either Tameran Wiccan or even Kemetic Reconstructionist audiences still tend to assume their readers participate in group or "temple" worship, often leaving solitary worshipers to adapt material as best they can. But in this chapter, solitary practice takes center stage. If you are already part of an Egyptian Pagan tradition of some kind, the basic, solar and lunar rites offered here are meant to give you more avenues to explore if you so choose. If you are an "Indie" Pagan, you will find not only rites for basic worship as well as adoration of the sun and moon, but also information on choosing a spiritual name and even performing a self-initiation in order to dedicate yourself to your chosen path. The material presented here primarily takes a Kemetic Reconstructionist format, in that it is based on ancient texts without adapting to an outside format; but Tameran Wiccans can also refer to the Correspondences and Quarter Calls section at the end of this chapter.

Iru - The Basic Rite

First explained in Following the Sun: A Practical Guide to Egyptian Religion, the basic *Iru* (literally 'Things Done') ritual is a simple form of observance that can be used for ordinary practice. It takes the form of an offering rite to one's chosen deities. If you need help with building an altar or choosing statues of your Gods or Goddesses, you can consult "Building - And Using - Your Own Sacred Space" in Following the Sun, as well as the *Kemetic How-to Guide* episodes "Building a Sacred Space" and "About Icon Statues".

The core *Iru* can be added to or incorporated in various ways, as we shall explore further. Consider it a building block from which larger constructions can be made.

Basic *Iru*:

Begin by lighting your candle(s) and ringing your sistrum, if you have one. Use this as a quiet moment, to signal your mind and body that it is time to slow down and relax.

Water: Pour water into the water cup.
Say: "Take these, Your cool waters that are the Inundation."

Milk: Pour milk into the milk cup.
Say: "Milk, milk, may You taste it in Your shrine."

Incense: Light incense. Hold up the stick or burner for a moment, to let some of it waft toward the icons.
Say: "I give You incense, I give You incense, great of purity."

Food: Place your food offering on its dish. Hold up the dish before the icons.
Say: "Take this, Your bread on which gods live."

Presentation of Offerings: Holding open your hands to the offerings, or gently motion over them with a wand or sistrum.

Say: "Turn Yourself to these, Your offerings; receive them from me."

Silent Prayer: This can be whatever you need it to be; quiet time for reflection or meditation, requests for things needed or for guidance, and so on. This time is between you and your Gods.

Closing: Use a ritual gesture, such as *henu* or one of its variations. This usually involves either raising your hands, palms-forward, even with your head and kneeling; or placing one hand to your chest, raising the other to head-height and kneeling on one knee. (For more ideas, log onto YouTube and check out "Henu and Gestures of Reverence" on *The Kemetic How-to Guide*.)

Say: "In-un-Ma'a [Truly it is]."

End of the rite

- *recitations based on Pyramid Texts 25, 199, 201, 459 and 460*

A basic rite such as Iru need not be elaborate. Author's photo.

The purpose of offering, of course, is to express our mutual relationship with the Gods. They have provided for us, so we offer back to Them as thanks and as our humble request that They continue to bless us. But what if you want to perform a longer or more involved ritual? Simply use the basic Iru as your core and build outward, such as in this longer version.

Long *Iru*

Lighting the Candle: As you light your candle(s), say:

"Come in peace, bright Eye of Horus, come in peace. Receive the light.
The Eye of Horus shines, like Ra in the twin Horizons, and evil hides before it. Receive the light.
The Eye of Horus destroys the enemies of Ra in all of their abodes. Receive the light.
The Eye of Horus comes, and I am purified with it. Receive the light."

- *from the Daily Rite of Amun-Ra, Karnak, and Book of the Dead chapter 137B*

Invocation to the Gods: Ring your sistrum, if you have one. Use a four-fold invocation to the deity (or deities) you are addressing; here it helps to be familiar with some of their titles. Refer to Appendix A for some common titles, or just use a simpler address such as below.

"Come in peace, oh *name of the god*, come in peace!" **or:**

"Hail unto You, oh *name of the god*, Lord (Lady) of Life, Lord (Lady) of Love!"

Offering Rite: The same as basic *Iru* -

Water: Pour water into the water cup.
Say: "Take these, Your cool waters that are the Inundation."

Milk: Pour milk into the milk cup.
Say: "Milk, milk, may You taste it in Your shrine."

Incense: Light incense. Hold up the stick or burner for a moment, to let some of it waft toward the icons.
Say: "I give You incense, I give You incense, great of purity."

Food: Place your food offering on its dish. Hold up the dish before the icons.
Say: "Take this, Your bread on which gods live."

Presentation of Offerings: Holding open your hands to the offerings, or gently motion over them with a wand or sistrum.
Say: "Turn Yourself to these, Your offerings; receive them from me."

Prayer: This can be your time for silent prayer, meditation, and so on. You can also use a hymn, such as one of the ones in Chapter Six, "Hymns to the Notjeru", or something of your own creation.

Closing: Ring your sistrum again, and perform a genuflection such as *henu*.
Say: "In-un-Ma'a [Truly it is]."

End of the rite

Note: Many Kemetic Reconstructionist rites call for a "Removing the Foot" or "Bringing the Foot" ceremony to close the rite, which involves backing away from the shrine while symbolically sweeping away one's footprints. While this procedure was commonly done in temples during pharaonic times, we have no evidence of it from private homes. As *Iru* is meant to be done at a home shrine and echo the spirit of private Egyptian worship, temple-specific actions such as "Removing the Foot" are not included.

Adoration of the Sun

"You shall pray to the Aten when he rises,
Saying: 'Grant me well-being and health';
He will give you your needs for this life,
And you will be safe from fear."
- *The Instructions of Amunemopet*

In the days before cell phones, alarm clocks, digital watches, and the myriad other techno-widgets we depend upon today, our predecessors timed their lives by natural cycles. Generally speaking, pre-Industrial peoples arose with the sun. When it was light, it was time to work. When the sun went down, less work could be done, so people geared down before going to sleep. Small wonder that the ancient Egyptians saw the sun god Ra as the creator of order and cyclical time.

Dawn in ancient Egypt was a sacred time. Sunrise meant that Ra, as the scarab or sun-child Khepri, had successfully harrowed the Underworld and thus Creation could renew itself. In the ancient Nile valley, animals and birds began to stir at sunup, especially the Cynocephalus baboons which were then common to the region. Their habit of gathering in the early morning sun to warm up, calling to one another in shrill cries that sounded like a language unto their own, must have been quite familiar to the ancient Egyptians. They came to associate these baboons with sunrise so closely that when they built open-air sun chapels into their temple complexes, they placed immense statues of baboons at each corner, their paws upraised in adoration. These baboons symbolized not only worship of Ra, but also an avatar of the god Djehuty (Thoth), who reckoned the hours and acted as Ra's deputy.

The most important of the daily rituals performed in temples was the morning ritual, which was observed as the sun emerged over the horizon. Outside the temples, many average Egyptians probably also emerged from their mud-brick houses to warm up and stretch in the morning sun. Clues in their language, literature and art suggest that an integral part of Egyptians' "morning ritual" was prayer. Their word for "morning", *duau*, has the same root as the word for "adoration" or "worship", *dua*. The texts and vignettes, or illustrations, comprising the Book of the Dead feature repeated scenes of adoration and hymns to 'Ra at his rising'. Often spells in magical papyri include directions that they be performed at dawn. The Instructions of Amunemopet, quoted above, also advised (referring to Aten as the visible aspect of the sun god):

"Do not let him report to the Aten at His rising,
'A youth has reviled an old man'."
- *Ancient Egyptian Literature, vol. II*

Taken together, all of these references present us with the idea that to Egyptian thinking, morning was a special time when average worshipers could directly address Ra Himself.

Of course, our modern society has in many ways detached itself from nature's diurnal cycle. Anyone who's lived the "college lifestyle" has on at least a few occasions spent a caffeinated night in front of a computer or game console, only realizing at the break of dawn how tired they are! Even after college, some jobs demand working a 'graveyard shift' and thus for people to invert their days and nights. Taxing as these habits may be on our bodies, for many of us they are critical to grades or a livelihood. However, if you can find the opportunity to go outside and view either sunrise or sunset, doing so would provide an excellent time for prayer and worship. You don't have to go through a full *Iru* and light candles or offer food, though you can if you so desire and have the time. You can also simply pause and face the sun on your way to your car to head to work or school; after getting up - or before going to bed, as the case may be; while waiting for a bus; or even checking the mailbox. (Just remember not to look directly at the sun, to avoid damaging your eyes. In this case, reverence has its practicality!) Any 'quiet time' you can take out of the usual hustle and bustle of daily living will allow you to reconnect, even if only for a few moments, with life's natural rhythm and with your Gods as They accompany Ra in the cosmic cycle.

If you want to make a formal practice of Adoration of the Sun, some possible invocations are included. By its very nature, Adoration will involve working closely with either Ra in one of His avatars, or a related solar deity. Of the goddesses, Hathor was most closely associated with the sun until Greco-Roman times, when Isis took on many of Hathor's roles. Invocations to both goddesses are included.

Most of us are not at our most eloquent at the beginning of a day, so a set of simple prayers in English are given first. These address Ra in the morning, Ra-Horakhety at noon, and Ra-Atum at evening. If you prefer to work with a different deity, change the name and feminize “Lord” to “Lady” or “Mistress” if applicable. “Lord of Life” and “Lord of Love” are common titles for all deities and frequently found in hymns, but “Lord of the Nine” refers to the Ennead of gods worshipped at Heliopolis and is specific to Ra. Look for other titles specific to your chosen solar deity in the translations of Egyptian invocations below.

English Prayers:

"Hail and praise unto You, oh Ra, Lord of Life and Lord of Love! Grant me life, well-being and health; may my eyes perceive Your goodness and my heart receive Your wisdom."

“Hail and praise, oh Ra-Horakhety, Lord of the Nine, Lord of Life! Shine upon me as You course the sky, that I may bring You *ma’at* and cast out *isfet*.”

"Hail and praise unto You, Ra-Atum, Lord of Eternity, Lord of Life! Guard me from the Evil One through the hours of the night; may Your protection be before me and Your strength be within me."

Egyptian-Language Invocations

If you have the opportunity - and brainpower! - for a longer address to the sun, try using these Egyptian invocations. The Egyptian words are given in italics, with the English translation in brackets. If you need help pronouncing the Egyptian version, log onto YouTube and check out *The Kemetic How-To Guide* (links included in "Books and Online References").

The invocations take the form of *Iiu im hotep*, or “Come in peace”, but you can also switch this with *Dua*, meaning “Praise” or “Thanks be to”; or with *Inodj har-ek*, “Hail unto You” (masculine suffix) or *Inodj har-et* (feminine suffix).

Morning Address to Khepri:
Iiu im hotep Khepri, Ka-Mutef.
[Come in peace, Khepri, Bull of His Mother.]
Iiu im hotep Khepri, djoser-remen.
[Come in peace, Khepri, sweeping of shoulder.]
Iiu im hotep Khepri, notjer a'ah.
[Come in peace, Khepri, Greatest God.]
Iiu im hotep Khepri, nub hekenu.
[Come in peace, Khepri, golden of jubilation.]

Midday Address to Ra:
Iiu im hotep Ra, Hor-Akhety.
[Come in peace, Ra, the Horus of the Horizons.]
Iiu im hotep Ra, neb Pesdjet.
[Come in peace, Ra, Lord of the Ennead (or "Nine").]
Iiu im hotep Ra, notjer a'ah.
[Come in peace, Ra, Greatest God.]
Iiu im hotep Ra, khai hekenu.
[Come in peace, Ra, appearing in jubilation.]

Evening Address to Atum:
Iiu im hotep Atum, Imy-Nun.
[Come in peace, Atum, He Who is in Nun.]
Iiu im hotep Atum, hotep.
[Come in peace, Atum, at rest.]
Iiu im hotep Atum, neheh.
[Come in peace, Atum, eternally renewing.]
Iiu im hotep Atum, Nedj-der-ef.
[Come in peace, Atum, Limitless One.]

Alternate Address: Elder Horus
Iiu im hotep Horu, Ba Iabty.
[Come in peace, Horus, Soul of the East.]
Iiu im hotep Horu, Akhety.
[Come in peace, Horus, He of the Horizons.]
Iiu im hotep Horu, neb pet.
[Come in peace, Horus, lord of the sky.]
Iiu im hotep Horu, notjer a'ah.
[Come in peace, Horus, Greatest God.]

Alternate Address: Amun-Ra

Iiu im hotep Amun-Ra, notjer a'ah.
[Come in peace, Amun-Ra, Greatest God.]
Iiu im hotep Amun-Ra, Nisut notjeru.
[Come in peace, King of the Gods.]
Iiu im hotep Amun-Ra, neb Waset.
[Come in peace, Lord of Thebes.]
Iiu im hotep Amun-Ra, neb khau.
[Come in peace, Lord of Appearances.]

Alternate Address: Hathor

Iiu im hotep Hat-Hor, notjerit a'ah.
[Come in peace, Greatest Goddess.]
Iiu im hotep Hat-Hor, nebet nub.
[Come in peace, Lady of Gold.]
Iiu im hotep Hat-Hor, nebet pet.
[Come in peace, Mistress of the Sky.]
Iiu im hotep Hat-Hor, nebet Yunit.
[Come in peace, Mistress of Denderah.]

Alternate Address: Isis

Iiu im hotep Iset, notjerit a'ah.
[Come in peace, Greatest Goddess.]
Iiu im hotep Iset, nebet pet.
[Come in peace, Mistress of the Sky.]
Iiu im hotep Iset, Uret Hikau.
[Come in peace, Great of Magic.]
Iiu im hotep Iset, nebet Pi-lak.
[Come in peace, Mistress of Philae.]

Feasts of the Moon

Integral as the solar cycle was to the ancient Egyptians, they considered the lunar cycle just as important. The moon represented various themes: it was Ra's gift, via Djehuty, to humankind so that they would not have to face every night in total darkness. It was the Sound Eye of Horus, waning because of Seth's injury to it before waxing healthy again. It was Khonsu, born with the first crescent, growing to adulthood in the full moon, aging and dying as it waned and then being conceived again on the night of the new moon. Sometimes the moon became the daughter of Ra, raging in the wilderness before returning to fullness again in Her father's company. Each of these themes was celebrated in various regions at various times, sometimes concurrently.

Egyptian temples charted the lunar cycle assiduously, and had particular rites for each day of the month based on the moon's phases. With the aid of modern astronomy, scholars have done very complicated studies of Egyptian lunar calendars, especially ones dating from the Ptolemaic era. Fortunately, for our purposes here a more general overview of major lunar observances will service well.

Each Egyptian lunar month begins on the new moon and ends on the day before the next new moon. To find dates and times for the lunar phases in your region, almanac.com provides an excellent resource. You can also find major phases listed in many wall calendars.

The following lunar observances are attested from numerous sources, ranging from memorial stelae to temple inscriptions to the Book of the Dead, and can be easily plotted with a modern calendar:

Pesdjentiu (New Moon) - Marking the beginning of a new month, this was an important observance. Bouquets of flowers were presented in temples, and offerings were made to the blessed dead. Chapters 135 and 141 of the Book of the Dead call for prayers, offerings and recitations to be made on the feast of the new moon. Its name as reconstructed from Ptolemaic temple records, *Pesdjentiu* or *Pesdjetu*, refers to the Ennead of Heliopolis (Iunu), possibly as symbolic of wholeness and totality.

A'bed (First Crescent) - The appearance of the first crescent marked the second day of the month, and the birth of the local lunar deity or the beginning of the Sound Eye's reappearance. *A'bed* means 'month', and this day was also called *Tep A'bed*, or 'Top of the Month'.

Senut (Sixth-Day Feast) - Six days into the month, Senut comes just before first quarter moon. Closely related to the Osirian cycle and Horus' Sound Eye, this lunar feast found frequent mention in memorial stelae. Floral bouquets were also presented in temples for Senut, and offerings were made to Osiris and the blessed dead. The Sound Eye's role as a symbol of filial offerings and resurrection figured primarily into the observance.

Medj-diunit (Full Moon) - The precise name for the full moon feast is somewhat uncertain, but some scholars read it as the 'Fifteenth-Day Feast', or *Medj-Diunit*. (More questionable is the rendering *Tep Semdet.*) Obviously this marked the high point of the month, when the Sound Eye was whole, the moon god was at the height of his powers, and the Eye of Ra was reunited with her father. It was also a time to make offerings, as many memorial stelae request offerings to be made the deceased owners on the 'Fifteenth-Day Feast'.

Denit (Last Quarter) - *Denit* actually referred to both the first and last quarter phase of the moon, or the seventh and twenty-third days of the month respectively. (True first quarter tends to vary, due to fluctuations in the moon's orbit, but it usually falls seven to eight days after new moon.) The meanings of these two days are more obscure, although frequent mention is made in the Coffin Texts of offerings 'on the sixth-day and seventh-day feasts', which would include first *Denit*. Last quarter may have reflected a similar meaning.

Peret Min (Last Crescent) - With the moon about to disappear, the month was drawing to a close. *Peret Min*, the 'Going Forth of Min', seems to refer to Min as an aspect of Horus, protecting his father Osiris. Here the moon takes on more of the role of Osiris, in a latent state in need of guarding before being re-conceived on the next night. From the perspective of the Eye of Ra, the goddess was at her most distant, ranging far in the desert before being enticed home again.

The Lunar Rites

The rites given below are structured around the basic *Iru*. Invocations are given for both male and female aspects of the moon, so that you can better adapt them to your own needs. If you plan to use them for Tameran Esbats, try incorporating one of the Tameran Quarter calls given at the end of this chapter to open and close your circle.

Pesdjentiu - New-Moon Feast

(Light your candles, ring your sistrum if you have one.)

"Open, Clouds! The dimmed Eye of Ra is covered, and Horus proceeds daily in joy, Great of Shape and Weighty of Power, to dispel dimness of the eye with His fiery breath. Behold, Oh Ra, I have come sailing, for I am one of those four gods at the corners of the sky, and I show you He who is present by day. Make Your rigging fast, for there is no opposition to You."
- adapted from Chapter 135 of the Book of the Dead

Alternate Invocation:
"Hail, Isis, Great Goddess, oh Giver of Life!
As Sopdut, You release the Inundation.
You give offerings to the gods and voice-offerings to the *akhu*.
As Mistress of Heaven, Earth and *Duat*, You watch over Your son Horus and brother Osiris."
- *adapted from the hymns to Isis at Philae*

(ring sistrum)

Offering Rite: *(use this to honor your personal gods)*

Water: "Take these, Your cool waters that are the Inundation."
Milk: "Milk, milk, may You taste it in Your shrine."
Incense: "I give You incense, I give You incense,
great of purity."
Food: "Take this, Your bread, on which gods live."

(ring sistrum)

"An offering of bread, beer, beef and fowl, incense and all good and pure things on which a god lives, to Osir, Khentiamentiu; to Ra-Horakhety; to the Great and Little Enneads; to the Seven Hat-Hors and the Bull of the West; to the Goodly Rudders at the four corners of the sky; to the Four Sons of Horus; to all the Gods in all their places; all the Guardians of Duat; and to the *ka*'s of these beloved *akhu*: [speak names of deceased being honored] ."

- *from Chapter 141 of the Book of the Dead*

Presentation: Turn Yourself to these, Your offerings; receive them from me.
(ring sistrum)

Prayer: Use this time to reflect and spend time with your gods.

In-un-Ma'a [Truly it Is]

A'bed - First Crescent

(Light your candles, ring your sistrum if you have one.)

"Hail to the Child in the Crescent!
He comes forth in His Majesty
As Khonsu, the Merciful, Who reckons the months;
As Djehuty, the True Scribe of Ma'at.
His mother is the Great Flood;
He grows, He flourishes,
He stands tall like His father."

Alternate Invocation:
"Hail, oh Mut, Mistress of All the Gods!
You bore Khonsu of Your essence
And suckled Him with Your sweetness.
Mistress of the Sky, Mistress of the Two Lands,
Shining One, Mother of the Crescent,
Hear this praise and rejoice!"
- both invocations adapted from Coffin Text 334

(ring sistrum)

Offering Rite: *(use this to honor your personal gods)*
Water: "Take these, Your cool waters that are the Inundation."
Milk: "Milk, milk, may You taste it in Your shrine."
Incense: "I give You incense, I give You incense,
great of purity."
Food: "Take this, Your bread, on which gods live."

Presentation: Turn Yourself to these, Your offerings; receive them from me.
(ring sistrum)

Prayer: Use this time to reflect and spend time with your gods.

In-un-Ma'a [Truly it Is]

Senut - Sixth-Day Feast

(Light your candles, ring your sistrum if you have one.)

"Hail, Osir! Repeated, renewed and refreshed is Your name of Un-nofer, Ra is Your power, Unti is what You are called!
You are in abundance, greatest of the gods, widespread of sweet savor among all who are not ignorant of You. Your war-cry is fierce, Oh swiftest of the Ennead, You who are stronger, more *ba* and more effective than the gods of Upper and Lower Egypt and their powers."

- *from Chapter 136A of the Book of the Dead*

Alternate Invocation:
"Oh Mighty Isis who protects Her brother, Great of Magic who drives off the foes! Clever of speech, whose words fail not, effective is Your command. You see Osiris' beauty in the Eye of Horus, in His name of Lord of Senut!"

- *adapted from the hymn to Osiris on the stela of Amenmose*

(ring sistrum)

Offering Rite: *(use this to honor your personal gods)*
Water: "Take these, Your cool waters that are the Inundation."
Milk: "Milk, milk, may You taste it in Your shrine."
Incense: "I give You incense, I give You incense, great of purity."
Food: "Take this, Your bread, on which gods live."

Voice offering:

Peret kheru, ta, heneket, kha khau, apdu, senotjer, merhat, khut nebet nofret wabet ankhet notjer im, en kau en..... [speak names of deceased being honored]*....ma'a-kheru her notjer a'ah.*

"A voice offering of bread, beer, a thousand of beef and poultry, incense and oil, and all good and pure things on which a god lives, for the *ka*s of _______, true of voice before the Great God."

Presentation: Turn Yourself to these, Your offerings; receive them from me.
(ring sistrum)

Prayer: Use this time to reflect and spend time with your gods.

In-un-Ma'a [Truly it Is]

Medj-Diunet - Full-Moon Feast

(Light your candles, ring your sistrum if you have one.)

"Hail, Djehuty, True Scribe of the Ennead,
Who reckons the months, the days, the hours,
Who restores the Sound Eye to fullness.
You return the Eye of Ra
To Her place on the brow of Her father,
And the Ennead of the Gods rejoices."
– *inspired by Book of the Dead chapters 95, 140 and 182*

Alternate Invocation:
"Hail, oh Hathor, oh Powerful One,
Shining Lady, Great of Flame!
You rest on the brow of Your father,
The gods support You in joy!
Shine forth as You did at the First Time,
Shine forth, complete and content!"
- adapted from the hymns to Hathor at Denderah

(ring sistrum)

Offering Rite: *(use this to honor your personal gods)*
Water: "Take these, Your cool waters that are the Inundation."
Milk: "Milk, milk, may You taste it in Your shrine."
Incense: "I give You incense, I give You incense,
great of purity."
Food: "Take this, Your bread, on which gods live."

Voice offering:

Peret kheru, ta, heneket, kha khau, apdu, senotjer, merhat, khut nebet nofret wabet ankhet notjer im, en kau en..... [speak names of deceased being honored]*....ma'a-kheru her notjer a'ah.*

"A voice offering of bread, beer, a thousand of beef and poultry, incense and oil, and all good and pure things on which a god lives, for the *ka*s of _______, true of voice before the Great God."

Presentation: Turn Yourself to these, Your offerings; receive them from me.
(ring sistrum)

Prayer: Use this time to reflect and spend time with your gods.

In-un-Ma'a [Truly it Is]

Denít - Last Quarter

(Light your candles, ring your sistrum if you have one.)

"Hail, Djehuty whose hands are pure,
Who dispels the darkness and quiets storm.
Ending the tumult and casting out evil.
Foretelling tomorrow, foreseeing the future,
You guide those in Heaven, Earth and Duat."
- adapted from Book of the Dead chapter 182

Alternate Invocation:
"Come, oh Golden One,
Come, Hathor, Sovereign Lady!
Cool Your heart, dispel Your anger,
Take joy in sistrum and song!
Come to the gods and come to the people,
Return with Your generous heart!"
- inspired by the Hathor hymns at Denderah

(ring sistrum)

Offering Rite: *(use this to honor your personal gods)*
Water: "Take these, Your cool waters that are the Inundation."
Milk: "Milk, milk, may You taste it in Your shrine."
Incense: "I give You incense, I give You incense, great of purity."
Food: "Take this, Your bread, on which gods live."

Presentation: Turn Yourself to these, Your offerings; receive them from me.
(ring sistrum)

Prayer: Use this time to reflect and spend time with your gods.

In-un-Ma'a [Truly it Is]

Peret Min - Last Crescent

(Light your candles, ring your sistrum if you have one.)

"Hail, Min, lofty of plumes,
Lord of Gebju who guards the moon!
Horus of the strong arm,
Min of upraised arm,
You banish evil and silence strife!
Protect the moon and protect the land
As you did for your father Osiris!"
- *adapted from the Hymn to Min, stela of Sobek-Iry*

(ring sistrum)

Alternate Invocation:
"Hail, oh Isis, Protectress of Osiris,
Who searched for Him unwearying!
Not resting until You found Him,
You gave Him breath with Your wings.
You received Him and bore His son,
Raised Him in places unknown.
Protect the moon and protect the land
as You did for Osiris and Horus!"
- *adapted from the hymn to Osiris on the stela of Amenmose*

Offering Rite: *(use this to honor your personal gods)*
Water: "Take these, Your cool waters that are the Inundation."
Milk: "Milk, milk, may You taste it in Your shrine."
Incense: "I give You incense, I give You incense,
great of purity."
Food: "Take this, Your bread, on which gods live."

Voice Offering:

Peret kheru, ta, heneket, kha khau, apdu, senotjer, merhat, khut nebet nofret wabet ankhet notjer im, en kau en..... [speak names of deceased being honored]*....ma'a-kheru her notjer a'ah.*

"A voice offering of bread, beer, a thousand of beef and poultry, incense and oil, and all good and pure things on which a god lives, for the *ka*s of _______, true of voice before the Great God."

Presentation: Turn Yourself to these, Your offerings; receive them from me.
(ring sistrum)

Prayer: Use this time to reflect and spend time with your gods.

In-un-Ma'a [Truly it Is]

Choosing an Egyptian Name

Pagans have commonly, though not universally, adopted the custom of choosing a craft name or 'magickal name' as part of their initiation into a path. This practice has in turn found use among Egyptian Pagans and Kemetics; some groups, for example, combine a divination of patron (or matron) deities with assigning an Egyptian name as part of their primary initiation. Their rationale, one echoed by Wiccans, is that a new name signifies a new identity, a new 'birth'.

This idea perhaps goes back to the Greco-Roman mystery religions, especially the Eleusinian mysteries, in which an initiate “died” to their old way of life so that they could be “reborn” into a more religious one. In a modern twist, “born-again” Christians use much the same reasoning. But ironically, this concept does not have any native Egyptian parallels. Deities and people (especially the pharaoh) added new names to represent new aspects of their personae, but older aspects were never replaced. So for Tamerans or Kemetics considering adopting an Egyptian name to reflect their practice, it might be best to keep this reasoning in mind; we are not *reborn* as much as we take on new *aspects* whenever we undertake a new chapter in our lives, such as a new faith.

So that you can better choose your own Egyptian name and shape your own persona, below you will find some basic Egyptian grammar tips and vocabulary. Whether you share your name with others, use it as an online handle, or keep it secret for your own spiritual practice - remember that the Egyptians regarded secret names as extremely potent - it will have strength because you chose it for yourself. To choose a name of our own is to make an assertion about our own individuality and autonomy, which is itself a gift from the Gods.

Rules of the Road: Egyptian Grammar

Didn't you hate sitting though grammar class, conjugating verbs and diagramming sentences *ad nauseum*? Well, those skills come in handy when working with other languages. Brush up on your sentence parts if needs be, because these basic rules of Egyptian grammar will help you construct a more coherent name.

1. *Verb suffixes indicate gender, person and tense.* Much of what English indicates with pronouns such as 'he' or 'she', and clarifying words such as 'has' or 'will', Egyptian accomplishes with suffixes added to the root verb. Person and tense can get a bit complicated. If you'd like to learn more about those, How To Read Egyptian Hieroglyphs by Mark Collier and Bill Manley is an ideal starting point. For our purposes, we will concentrate on gender in the third person, which is most commonly found in names. The suffix *-ef* is masculine, indicating a male subject; *-es* is feminine, indicating a female subject.

Example: *Djed-ef* The root verb is *djed*, meaning "say" or "speak"; *-ef* is the suffix, equating to English "he". Hence, "he says". You might recognize this combination in the name *Hordjedef*, one of the sons of King Khufu, which essentially means, "Horus speaks". (Alternatively, according a more complicated rule of Egyptian grammar, it could also mean something ongoing: "What Horus says".) The feminine equivalent would be *djed-es*, "she says", although names using this combination for a goddess seem to be fairly rare.

You may see names like Hordjedef in reverse order, as *Djedefhor*; the same issue appears with the name of Hordjedef's brother, Radjedef - also known as *Djedefre*. Another example would be *Nakhtmin*, a.k.a. *Minnakht* ["Min is strong"]. The reason for this is because written Egyptian honorifically places gods' names first, despite whatever the original pronunciation may have been. Some scholars keep the honorific placement, others don't, hence the confusion.

2. *Verb first, then subject.* As seen with #1, Egyptian syntax uses a different order than the subject-verb-object we follow in English. Generally speaking (there are exceptions), Egyptian gives the verb first, then the subject of the verb, followed by the object.

Example 1: *Mer-es-Aset* [hyphens are added so you can see the component words] *Mer*, "loves", is the verb; *-es* is the feminine suffix, indicating "she"; *Aset* is the object. Hence, "She loves Isis [Aset]".

Example 2: *Djed-Khonsu-ef-ankh* This is a slightly harder one. Here *djed* is the main verb, "says". *Khonsu* is the subject; *-ef* refers to the object, in this case the person. *Ankh*, of course, means "live". Put together, this name forms a short sentence, "Khonsu says he [will] live." The feminine equivalent of the name is *Djed-Khonsu-es-ankh*, "Khonsu says she will live." Such names became fairly common in the Late Period, when parents would frequently seek oracles from deities about the welfare of their newborn children.

3. *Use prepositions and particles cautiously.* Egyptian particles seem at first glance to correspond directly with English prepositions, such as "of" or "in", but appearances are deceiving! *Em* is often translated as "in", and it can correlate to either "in" or "of"; but it carries the additional meaning of placement or state of being. *En*, on the other hand, corresponds to "of" in the possessive sense. *Pa* can also equate to "of", but it also seems to swap with *Pu*, which roughly equates to "is" or "this". Sound confusing? You do have one advantage: because their syntax is different, Egyptian does not use prepositions or particles nearly as often as English does. In fact, they had no words for, 'a', 'an', or even 'and'. You will see examples of names below that give good indications of where particles are used and where the meaning doesn't require them.

First Word Bank: Major Egyptian Deity Names

Where the modern name differs from the original Egyptian, the original language version is given in italics.

Anubis *Anpu*
Amun
Aton
Bastet
Bes
Geb
Hathor *Hat-Hor* or *Hut-Heru*
Horus *Hor(u) or Heru*
Isis *Aset or Iset*
Ihy
Khonsu
Khnum
Min
Mut
Nut
Osiris *Osir* or *Ausir*
Ptah
Ra
Sakhmet
Selket *Serqet*
Shu
Seth *Sutekh* or *Suti*
Tefnut
Thoth *Djehuty*
Wepwawet *Wep* [or *Up*]-*waut*

Second Word Bank: Egyptian Terms and Combinations

The term in Egyptian is given first, in italics, followed by its feminine variation and then its English translation. An ellipsis (...) indicates where the name of a deity would be placed.

Bak / Baket ... = Servant of ...
Sa / Sat ... = Son / daughter of ...
Meri / Merit ... = Beloved of ...
Mer-ef / Mer-es ... = Loving ...
Pa ... = One of ...

(Note: This name type survives, in derivitive form, in Egyptian Arabic as *Bahur* ["One of Horus"] and *Banub* ["One of Anubis"].)

Djed ... efankh / esankh = ... says he /she will live
... *emsa-ef / -es* = He / She is in ...'s protection
... *emwia* = ... in His (Her) Sacred Barque
... *mose* = Born of ...
... *hotep* = ... is content
... *nakht* = ... is strong
... *emhab* = ... is in feast
... *nofer / nofrit* = ... is good
... *woser / wosret* = ... is powerful
... *nodjem / nodjmit* = ... is sweet
... *emhat* = ... is foremost
... *uben* [or *weben*] = ... rises
... *a'ah* = ... is great (or greatest)
... *shepses / shepsut* = ... is noble
Qai ... = ... is exalted
Shedi ... = Whom ... rears
Inedju (en) ... = Whom ... saves
Neb / Nebet ... = ... is Lord / Lady
variation: ... *paneb / panebet*
Ni-ankh ... = ... possesses life (or Living in ...)

Third Word Bank: Non-Theophoric Names

Not all Egyptian names are *theophoric*, meaning they incorporate the name or title of a deity.

Senebi / Senebit = Health, wellness
Nakht = Strength (generally a masculine name)
Nofrit = Beauty, goodness (feminine)
Meri / Merit = One of love (or loving one)
Neb- / Nebetqed = Man (or woman) of character
Neferronpet = Good year
Neferhotep = Good offering (or Beautiful peace?)

These names are non-theophoric, but also fairly well-known to Egyptian history, so use your own discretion:

Yuya	*Aya*	*Inyuya*
Tjuyu	*Maya*	*Raya*
Kiya	*Sennedjem*	

We'll skip the obvious *Nefertiti, Nefertari* and *Imhotep.*

Self-Initiation

No one has yet found a tablet inscribed with hieroglyphs that read, "You must be initiated in order to worship Egyptian gods". In all probability, nobody ever will. Formal initiations in ancient Egypt seem to have been limited to high-ranking priests and, of course, the king. But today, initiation forms an integral part of the Wiccan degree system and has been adapted into many other Pagan traditions as well. Many Solitaries also choose to perform a self-initiation as a way of formalizing their chosen path. So while it should not be considered a 'must', if you do decide to undertake a self-initiation, it can serve as a sincere expression of personal faith.

What Should I Wear?

In some Pagan circles this question would be emended to, "Should I wear anything at all?" These Pagans embrace 'skyclad' practice as an affirmation of their own bodies; meanwhile, critics point out that Gerald Gardner, essentially the founder of Wicca, was also an avid nudist who incorporated nudity into his coven tradition. When it comes to Egyptian Pagan practice, the choice ultimately rests with the practitioner. Ancient sources do suggest that nudity, while not regarded as negatively as it is today, was more acceptable for children than for adults. Children were usually pictured naked in reliefs, sculptures and paintings. After puberty, clothing seemed to be the rule even in festival settings. One woman in Deir el-Medina even wrote to her sister, "Weave for me that shawl very promptly before Amenhotep [deified pharaoh who was the village patron] comes [in procession], because I am really naked. Make one for my backside because I am naked"!

What scant (forgive the pun) references we have for initiations suggest that they involved the initiate wearing a loincloth - being in their underwear, if you will. They were probably ceremonially 'bathed' with water poured from ceremonial vessels (this motif occurs often in relation to coronations as well) and then vested with garments indicating their office. This included crowns and scepters in the case of the king.

So if you opt not to work 'skyclad', your next question might be, "What color should I wear?" White is the hue that we most often associate with Egyptian clothing, and indeed white tends to be preferred by Kemetic practitioners. Do not discount the use of color, however. The Egyptians had their own unique color associations which you can incorporate into your ritual garb. Refer to the "Correspondences" section below for a list of color associations.

The example rite given below is meant for consecration to a patron or matron deity. If you have more than one (which is quite common), simply use plurals where appropriate.

A Self-Initiation Rite

I. Purification

Shave and bathe prior to the ritual according to your own particular method. Fasting is optional. If consecrating to Osiris, Isis or Horus, you may want to avoid eating pork or fish, or else ritually purify yourself afterward. Let your intuition be your guide.

Set up your altar, if you will be performing the initiation outside of your own private altar space. You will need a basin or bowl of water (and probably a towel) for the ritual purification.

Put on your ceremonial garb. For a basic initiation, it can be either white or another color; for a priest-level initiation, white is preferred. Light altar candles and ring your sistrum, if using one, to begin the rite.

Say: "Hail to You, Great God(dess)! I have come to You, my Lord (Lady), that I may see Your beauty, for I know You and I know Your name. Behold, I have come before You, oh _____, I bring you *ma'at* and I repel *isfet* for You." – *from Book of the Dead chapter 125*

Anoint your head and hands with water from the basin. This will probably be as simple as just leaning your head over the bowl, dipping your hands in and pouring the water over your head. Again, you might want to keep a towel handy!

Say: "I have cast out all evil that is within me. I am pure, I am pure, I am pure, I am pure."

2. Eating Bread

Perform a standard offering rite to your chosen deities - refer to the basic *Iru* or use your own. Afterward, hold up bread (cakes, or other food items) before the deities.

Say: "Of what shall I eat? I shall eat the bread which Rennutet provides for me in the shrine of the gods. I shall eat of bread and partake of truth [*ma'at*]."

Eat the bread and drink the milk or wine, but save the water for the final step.

3. Consecration

Using your pinkie finger, anoint your forehead with oil. If you will be using a piece of jewelry or vestment to ritually signify your initiation, place it on at this time.

Say: "Hail to You, oh _________, in all Your names and in all Your places! Place Your consecration upon me. May You make it beneficial to me, and may You protect me from all evil.

"Receive me and place Your arms over me, for I am Your *shemsu* ["follower"; if adopting an Egyptian name, use it here] upon this earth. May I be beneficial to You and to humankind, as You are beneficial to me."

Variation if using a vestment: "...in all Your names and in all Your places! Grant this pure vestment [or, 'pure office of ______'] upon me. May You make it beneficial to me..."

4. Closing

Ring the sistrum, if using one. Drink the water from the offerings to signal the end of the rite.

Say: "*In-un-ma'a.*" [Truly it is]

Correspondences

The ancient Egyptians differed from the ancient Greeks in that they did not perceive the world as comprising five elements. Similarly, associations between colors, stones or other materials and esoteric properties come from Neo-Platonism and are not native to Egyptian belief. But correspondences are frequently used in Wiccan practice, so for the benefit of Tameran Wiccans seeking more historically-based references, some basic properties of colors, herbs, and stones according to ancient Egyptian thought are given below.

Colors

The ancient Egyptians did not see colors quite the same way that we do. For example, we would say that the Mediterranean Sea is blue, but the Egyptian name for it meant "Great Green"! In spite of their different descriptors, however, we can deduce certain attributes for certain colors or groups of colors.

Red, Yellow and Orange – All three colors could be described by the same word. Yellow and orange in wall paintings signified gold (see "Stones and Metals", below), and like gold were associated with solar deities. Red was very much a "power color", though. It could signify aggressive strength, danger, the desert (hence its name "Red Land"), evil or the warding off of evil. Red was associated with the god Seth, but also Eye of Ra goddesses such as Hathor, Tefnut and Sakhmet.

Green – In a desert land, green was life. Green symbolized vegetation and all properties associated with it: abundance, growth, flourishing, renewal and rebirth. In fact, an Egyptian expression for making someone prosper was to "make them green" – quite the opposite of our modern sayings "green with envy" or "turning green" with sickness! Osiris' often green skin indicated his supreme powers of renewal and rebirth, for people as well as crops.

Blue – Naturally, blue suggested water and the sky; which the Egyptians saw as related, since Ra sailed his sun boat across the sky, and beyond the sky goddess Nut's body lay the chaotic waters of Nun. So, the color blue had aquatic and celestial connotations. Dark blue symbolized the night sky. Turquoise blue was particularly sacred to Hathor as a celestial goddess and Lady of the West. Blue-green, being much the same as spectrum green to Egyptian eyes, also suggested renewal.

The color purple existed in amethyst and other naturally-occurring substances, but was probably regarded as an extension of either dark blue or red, depending on hue. Its associations would match accordingly.

Black – The color of fertile soil and hence their nation, *Kemet* ("Black Land"), black also signified renewal. But black held an added connotation of magical efficacy. It was a favored color in *heka*, or Egyptian magic, followed by red. Black thread was often used for binding; the color as well as the knots put into the string gave the spell its power.

White - Most Egyptian clothing was made of linen, a material which resists dyes, so it was usually white. As a color, white suggested purity, as it does in many cultures. Interestingly, it also seemed to be a preferred color for funerals; many tomb paintings show mourners in plain white clothes and, in the case of Tutankhamun's funerary procession, plain white headbands as well. Being a religious occasion, the white may have suggested formality.

Herbs

The Egyptian pharmacopeia was renowned in the ancient world, but today some of the ancient Egyptian names for known species of plants remain untranslated. Serious herbalists are encouraged to obtain a copy of <u>An Ancient Egyptian Herbal</u> by Lise Manniche; it contains a wealth of information. What follows below is a brief selection of plants that have divine or magical associations.

Acacia – Tree species native to the African continent, connected with Sakhmet as the Eye of Ra.

Apple – A luxury import in pharaonic times, it was pictured in royal offerings to the Nile god Hapy.

Barley – Along with wheat, it was associated with Osiris.

Birthwort – A type of vine that had erotic and possible Hathoric connotations, often pictured in scenes of childbirth.

Blue lotus – Actually a species of blue lily, it symbolized rebirth and the sun god emerging at dawn. It was particularly sacred to the god Nefertum, and solar deities in general.

Bryony – White and black bryony, both toxic species of vine, were burned in execration rites.

Chick peas – Called "falcon's head beans" in ancient times, these were sacred to Horus the Child and presented to him on his feast day.

Cinnamon – An imported spice, it was used in incense and presented to Amun-Ra in temple reliefs. May have had solar associations based on this, but this has not been verified.

Fig, Sycamore Fig – These were associated with Hathor, "Mistress of the Sycamore".

Fleabane – Used to drive away pests, including crocodiles in the Underworld, according to the Book of the Dead!

Galbanum – An imported substance, used in incense.

Garlic – Its name formed a homonym with the word for "harm", so it was used in protective magic to ward off evil.

Ivy – Greek writers reported that ivy was sacred to Osiris, but modern scholars debate on which species of vine they called "ivy", since true ivy does not grow well in Egypt.

Lettuce – Specifically Romaine or Cos lettuce, it was sacred to Min and associated with male fertility. It was considered an aphrodisiac. Seth was said to favor lettuces, though in "The Contendings of Horus and Seth", his taste for lettuce backfired on him rather dramatically!

Because of its Sethian links, priests at Philae considered lettuce taboo.

Mandrake – Its fruit were associated with eroticism.

Onion – Having one part growing below ground and the rest reaching skyward, onion symbolized the ability to cross realms, making it sacred to Sokar. Young bulbs were also called the "white teeth of Horus"; Horus as well as Eye goddesses such as Bast seem to have had associations with onions.

Papyrus – The heraldric plant of Lower Egypt associated with the cobra goddess Wadjit, it also symbolized lushness and was associated with Hathor.

Persea – *Mimusops laurifolius*, a type of tree now found only in the southern Arabian peninsula and the Horn of Africa, the persea or *ished* tree was sacred to Ra and the Eye goddesses. A persea tree in Iunu (Heliopolis) was the site of Ra's triumph as a tomcat over the serpent Apophis.

Sweet Marjoram – This herb may have been the type used in a famed Egyptian perfume that was sacred to the god Sobek.

Watermelon – According to legend, Seth pursued Isis unsuccessfully as a bull. His spilled seed became watermelon plants. Hence watermelon has fertility and Sethian associations.

Wheat – Specifically emmer wheat, an ancient strain now grown as "farro" wheat for Italian cuisine, emmer was sacred to all the gods but particularly Osiris.

Stones and Metals

Keeping in mind that the Egyptians did not ascribe metaphysical properties to elements or colors, the properties they sought in stones were based largely upon color. They had no precious stones such as diamonds, rubies or sapphires. The semiprecious stones and precious metals below have been found in ample supply in ancient Egyptian relics:

Lapis Lazuli – A dark blue to grayish-blue stone imported from what is now Afghanistan, lapis lazuli has celestial associations and could symbolize rebirth. It was considered the "hair" of the gods.

Carnelian – A red to red-orange stone, carnelian was linked to goddesses, Isis in particular. It might have symbolized female fertility or potency.

Obsidian – Technically volcanic glass, this black stone was favored for used in ritual implements for its ability to take a sharp edge.

Malachite – Also called "greenstone" in translated texts, it suggested rebirth and may have been the material of Ra's sun bark (if Spell 133 of the Book of the Dead is representative). The Pyramid Texts refer to sashes of rank being made of malachite. Eyepaint of malachite was also worn on New Year's Day.

Faience – A manmade ceramic compound that fires to blue or blue-green color, faience held strong solar and Hathoric associations. Its name, *tjehen*, meant "dazzling".

Gold – Considered the "flesh of the gods", gold had a close link to Ra as well as Hathor. It symbolized eternal life because it never tarnishes.

Silver – A symbolically lunar metal to counter gold's solar aspects, silver was much rarer in Egypt.

Iron – Rarer still, iron was only available in pharaonic times in its meteoric form. It was strongly linked to Seth, but also the air god Shu. Hematite, a semiprecious stone possessing high iron content, can conceivably be interpolated as a Sethian stone.

Tameran Quarter Calls

As explained earlier, Egyptian rituals did not call for a circular space to be demarcated. But they did invoke the cardinal directions in certain spells or ritual actions, and associated specific deities with them. These can be adapted into a Tameran system with some adjustments; for example, the order they used varied, usually going either counter-clockwise (widdershins) or in a cross pattern, which does not correspond with the typical clockwise (doesil) circle used in Wicca.

The Four Sons of Horus: *(This version involves the callers sprinkling water and natron.)*

East: Duamutef (doo-AH-mew-tef), Adoring His Mother! You live on Ma'at and lean on your electrum staff as watchman of the East! You are purified with natron, you are purified with water.

West: Qebehsenuef (keb-uh-SEN-yew-ef), who Cools His Brothers! You live on Ma'at and lean on your electrum staff as watchman of the West! You are purified with natron, you are purified with water.

North: Hapy (hah-pee), He of Haste! You live on Ma'at and lean on your electrum staff as watchman of the North! You are purified with natron, you are purified with water.

South: Imsety (im-SET-ee), He of the Dill! You live on Ma'at and lean on your electrum staff as watchman of the South! You are purified with natron, you are purified with water."

- *adapted from Pyramid Text 573*

The Four Rudders of Heaven (*Going North, West, East, South*)

"Hail, Good Power, Beautiful Rudder of the Northern Sky."
"Hail, Circler of Heaven, Guide of the Two Lands, Beautiful Rudder of the Western Sky."
"Hail, Transfigured One Before the Temples of the Gods, Beautiful Rudder of the Eastern Sky."
"Hail, Foremost Before the Temple Sands, Beautiful Rudder of the Southern Sky."

- *from Book of the Dead Spell 148*

The Four Powers of Heaven (*Going widdershins North, West, South, East*)

"Hail, Gods Above the Earth, Guides of *Duat*."
"Hail, Divine Mothers Above the Earth, Who Are in the Necropolis and the House of Osiris."
"Hail, Gods, Guides of the Sacred Land, Who Are Above the Earth, Guides of *Duat*."
"Hail, Followers of Ra, Ones in the Suite of Osiris."

- *adapted from Book of the Dead Spell 148, Papyrus of Ani*

Even if you don't call Quarters in private rituals, it helps to be familiar with them in case you host an open ritual, as in this Feast of Osiris. Author's photo.

Heka

The Egyptian word *heka* generally equates to what we would call 'magic' - or more appropriately, what Pagans call 'magick'. But our modern understanding of 'magic' is somewhat different from the Egyptians' ideas about *heka*, and defining both terms satisfactorily has often bedeviled scholars. Why? To explain, we have to examine our ideas about 'magic' and how they relate to our notions of religion.

Magical 'Baggage'

Since the days of the Ptolemies, magic has held an exotic, mysterious, sometimes contraband connotation. "Magic" comes from the Greek word *magoi*, referring to practices that were associated with Persia and Zoroastrianism; hence the Three Wise Men of the Nativity story being referred to as the 'Magi'. The air of mystery and foreignness surrounding magic has been viewed both positively and negatively over the centuries. Even the ancient Hebrews had an ambivalent regard for it: Jeremiah 19:1-11 actually describes that prophet employing an execration rite involving the smashing of pottery, but the prophet Elijah denounced divination and other magical practices as blasphemies introduced to Judea with the worship of Baal. Later, as Christianity took root in the Roman world, early Coptic Christians wrote magical texts invoking Egyptian deities alongside Christ and the Virgin Mary at much the same time that key Apostles were writing letters to Aegean communities condemning any contact with pagan practices. Oddly enough, the pagan Roman emperors did as much as their Christianized successors to suppress various magical practices as subversive; Augustus Caesar, Tiberius, Claudius, Nero and other emperors all issued edicts banning foreign, "un-Roman" magical practices as fraudulent and illegal.

This Roman view of magic passed down to our Western society through centuries of church repression and anti-witchcraft laws. During the Victorian Era, when our modern sciences of anthropology and archaeology were still in their infancy, writers attempted to define magic as something separate from religion. James Frazier, author of The Golden Bough (which later influenced Wicca), defined magic as actions directly intended to obtain a specific result. By contrast, he stated that religion sought results more passively through divine intervention. This view is still widely held today. Magic was - and in many minds still is - considered the illegitimate sibling of religion, an underground practice carried out by unsanctioned elements of a given society. Now, of course, magic carries the additional association with famous illusionists such as Harry Houdini, David Copperfield and Criss Angel, who perform fantastic feats of spectacle for popular entertainment.

For this reason, Pagans spell the word for their own practices differently, to distinguish m-a-g-i-c-k from the more popularly recognized m-a-g-i-c. But our shared cultural attitudes persist; consider how many Pagans prefer to concentrate their activities on "Craft work" - magick - to the relative exclusion of worshiping patron deities. This separation of "Craft" and worship reflects mainstream society's continued perception that magic(k) and religious expression are distinctly different entities.

Defining *heka*

Attempting to draw the same dividing line amidst ancient Egyptian practices, however, quickly leads to a dead-end. Many of their rites simply cannot be put into neat categories of 'magical' versus 'devotional', because they contain aspects of both. Obviously magical spells meant to cure a person afflicted by a scorpion sting also involved reciting myths about either Ra and his goddess daughter or Isis and Horus. Observances for the feast days of gods commonly involved ritual, magical acts that commemorated or even assisted the actions of the deities being celebrated. Perhaps more confusingly, the same groups of texts that extolled deities also cajoled or even threatened them. The Pyramid Texts of King Unas, for example, contain both passages describing Unas being welcomed by the gods with open arms, and the Cannibal Hymn that describes Unas eating the gods and swallowing their *heka*!

Clearly, then, Egyptian *heka* does not match our idea of magic as something illusory or unorthodox. It does fall much more closely in line with the Pagan idea of magick, but it lacks the independence from devotional aspects that is sometimes sought in 'Craft'. Though frequently a morally ambivalent force, *heka* also forms an inseparable part of Egyptian religious practice and can be used by either gods or humankind. So what is *heka*?

Heka, like *ma'at*, issued from the Creator (or Creatrix, in the case of Neith). It took on personified form as a male god, Heka. As a force, *heka* was the power the Creator used to fashion the ordered world, the gods and humankind. Each of the gods had their own *heka*, and in the Instructions of King Merikara *heka* was given to humans "to ward off the blows of what might happen". *Heka* referred to the magical words used in spells as well as the power behind them. Egyptologist Erik Hornung aptly described *heka* as "the nuclear power of the ancient world", capable of either tremendous benefit or disastrous harm.

Ancient Egyptians applied this magical power to a wide variety of purposes; so much so that modern writers have sometimes concluded that they either were extremely paranoid and superstitious, or else that the 'folk religion' which practiced *heka* was vastly disconnected from the more 'lofty-minded' state religion. Neither conclusion is likely correct. When it comes to 'superstition', we are only so far removed from the Egyptians ourselves. Some people today refuse to go anywhere without checking their horoscope or pocketing their lucky rabbit's foot. Meanwhile, others look aghast on such practices as 'ungodly' but will buy something they don't need just to avoid having their bill total $6.66. And some modern vocations, particularly performing arts and professional sports, come with their own unique practices and folklore; such as tapping a team sign on the way out to the playing field, or wishing a stage actor good luck by saying, "Break a leg". Innocuous as these practices may seem, an ancient Egyptian observer would rightly call them our modern version of *heka*.

Types of *heka*

So what actions constitute *heka*? Broadly speaking, they can be divided into four types: protection and healing, controlling, execration and divination. Within each of these categories come a variety of techniques, which often overlap. For our purposes at hand, a few representative examples will be given for each. Those interested in more in-depth research can consult the Bibliography for further reading. But first, let us define the four types of *heka* more closely:

Protection and healing - A great deal of Egyptian magic is protective in nature. Their word for 'protection', *sa*, can also refer to protective amulets and magic. A practitioner of this type of magic was known as a *sau*, and one of their main specialties was making amulets. *Sau* were also considered medical experts, along with *sunu* (doctors) and *wa'b Sakhmet* (*wa'b* priests of Sakhmet). Because Egyptian medicine lacked our understanding of pathogens, they incorporated spells to cast out fever or disease demons and poison with physical remedies such as poultices, herbal decoctions and bandaging. They saw no contradiction between the two approaches.

Controlling - Some *heka* sought to influence people or inanimate objects. Egyptian folk tales are filled with descriptions of sorcerers using wax effigies or other models to control larger objects: one famous example from *Papyrus Westcar* involved a lector priest turning a clay model of a crocodile into a real one, which he then sent after his cheating wife and her lover!

Love spells also fall into the category of controlling magic. Typically they involve making a woman fall in love with a man. The earliest such spells, dating from the New Kingdom, demand amusingly, "make N born of N run after me like a cow after grass, like a herdsman after his flock!" Much more sinister is an effigy from a Roman-era love spell, now in Paris. A clay female figure, kneeling with her hands behind her, still has nails piercing her head, eyes, ears, mouth, hands, feet, heart and genitals. With it, the practitioner clearly sought absolute domination over the object of his lust.

Execration - Spells meant to cast out and destroy evil in various forms are known today as execration spells. These are not necessarily the same as *exorcism* rites, which deal exclusively with casting out evil spirits who are either possessing a person or haunting a location. In ancient times, execration spells were performed by state temples to defeat, through magical means, foreign enemies and dissidents. Other spells aimed to defend against cosmic forces of chaos, though in state rites these cosmic elements were combined with earthly enemies. Whether these 'secret rites' percolated from temples into the general community or first originated in everyday folk practices remains a matter of debate. But hexing an enemy became commonplace enough that a fate many Egyptians sought to avoid was 'death by potsherd', referring to a common execration technique. That same practice is still echoed today in the Egyptian Arabic expression, "break a pot behind him," said after an unsavory person leaves the room!

Divination - A prime example of why Egyptian magic cannot be wholly separated from Egyptian religion would be their divination practices. One of their most common forms of divination, documented from New Kingdom into Christian times, involved seeking a deity's decision (via their icon) between possible scenarios written on potsherds or papyrus 'tickets'. Movements of an icon statue in procession or the movements of a sacred animal such as the Apis bull were interpreted in another method of divination. A village "wise woman," or *ta rekhet*, was often called upon to interpret freak acts of nature which were seen to have divine origins. Dream interpretation served as another type of divination. By the Greco-Roman era people would enact elaborate spells in order to receive a vision and message from a deity in their dreams. Or they would practice incubation, in which they would pay to spend the night in a temple in order to receive a visit from the god.

Techniques of *Heka*

Egyptian spells are well-known from literature; less known but just as important are the actions and gestures that often accompanied spoken spells. Some techniques are described below, including types of *heka* into which they were often incorporated.

Knot-tying – Cords and ribbons were often used in spells to create protective barriers or to bind dangerous entities. Knots were most commonly used in groups of four or seven, both potent numbers in Egyptian belief, but some exceptional spells called for as many as 365. Black cord was preferred for many spells, and often held associations with Anubis. Red ribbons of the Seven Hathors (seven emanations of Hathor who had protective powers) were used to bind demons. Other spells called for images drawn on white linen, which was then knotted a prescribed number of times.

An extension of this idea can be found in Greco-Roman magical papyri; when a young boy participated in a necromancy spell, he wore an amuletic bracelet made of four white, four green, four blue and four red threads, stained with the blood of a hoopoe-bird and with a wrapped winged scarab attached, as a means of protection against hostile spirits.

One chapter from the Book of the Dead refers to knot-tying, and could be used in spell work:

Book of the Dead Chapter 50 - For Not Entering Into the Slaughterhouse of the God

"The four knots are tied about me by the guardian of the sky. He has made the knot firm for the Inert One [Osiris] on His thighs on that day of cutting off the lock of hair.

"The knot was tied about me by Seth, in whose power the Ennead were at first, before uproar had come into being, when He caused me to be well."

Alternatives could include invocations to Anubis or to the Seven Hathors. In a modern context, knot-tying could be used for protection against a variety of negative influences, nightmares or bad luck, or to seal something with negative energy in need of containment.

Hand-placement and gestures – The "laying of hands" is known throughout many cultures as a protective or healing gesture. In ancient Egypt another gesture referred to as *sa* (protection) involved pointing with the index finger and thumb. This occurs in tomb scenes where herdsmen move cattle across treacherous stretches of water; someone from the riverbank or the prow of a raft points in the *sa* gesture at the cattle, hoping to keep crocodiles pictured in the waters from marauding. (Some scholars debate the meaning of these scenes, but R. K. Ritner's The Mechanics of Ancient Egyptian Magical Practice argues compellingly that the pointing gesture is a means of magical protection.) A similar gesture, meant to seal out evil forces, used the index and middle fingers held straight together and touching the person or thing being sealed. Amulets shaped like these two fingers have been found in mummy wrappings.

Both Anubis and Amun-Ra were said to be able to protectively seal other gods or human beings to prevent evil from entering them. Invocations to either god would thus be appropriate choices for "sealing" magic. Another utterance comes from a spell to protect a child:

"My hand is on you, my seal is your protection."

Music, sound – Aside from pleasing the goddess Hathor, the jingling of sistrums also drove away evil. So too did dancing, clapping, and the stamping of feet. It's easy to imagine clapping or stamping feet accompanying these Utterances to drive away dangerous creatures which come from the Pyramid Texts:

"The cobra that came from the earth has fallen, the fire that came from Nun has fallen. Fall down, crawl away!" *PT 233*

"You of the evil deed, you of the evil deed! You of the wall, you of the wall! Set your foot behind you, set your arms behind you! Beware of the Great One!" *PT 380, PT 651*

Use of sistrums generally accompanied hymns, especially to Hathor. Sometimes the players identified themselves with Ihy, Hathor's son who was pictured naked and holding a sistrum. Inscriptions from Hathor's temple at Denderah include a Hymn to the Sistrum, part of which reads:

"I have taken the sistrum, I grasp the sistrum, I drive away one who is hostile to the Mistress of Heaven…I dispel what is evil by means of the sistrum which is in my hand."

Either technique can be used to dispel negativity, cleanse your home or bless a ritual space.

Use of herbs, materials – Most Egyptian medicine was herbal, and was included alongside incantations to heal people afflicted with sickness, snakebites or scorpion stings. Some herbs had more esoteric uses as well. One spell to protect a house against malevolent ghosts, snakes or scorpions called for garlic – which, in the Egyptian language, punned their word for 'harm' – to be pounded, mixed with beer, then sprinkled over the house at night. Accompanying spells probably included identifying the parts of the house with various deities (see *Naming, apotheosis* below).

Other materials were used to purify or create boundaries. Natron held powerful purifying properties, as evidenced in the Opening of the Mouth offerings which included natron. Sand could be used to purify, either by sprinkling or by burying something in it. Making a circle around an object with sand also formed a protective barrier.

Circumambulation – Related to encircling with sand or natron salt was tracing a circle with a wand, usually of ivory, or by walking in a circle around something (circumambulation). Encircling something symbolized possession or power over it; Ra circled the created world in his sun barge, the pharaoh's name was written in an oval cartouche which symbolized "all that the sun encircles", and deities such as Sokar circumambulated their city walls during festival times. As with knotting, circumambulation was frequently done four times.

Smashing, burning – Execration rites made extensive use of smashing and burning articles. As described above, the names of things (or people) meant to be banished were written on red clay pots which were then ritually smashed to pieces. In a much more elaborate state rite dated to the Old Kingdom, actual sculptures of prisoners-of-war were decapitated and shattered. In other rituals, either wax effigies or sheets of papyrus inscribed in red ink with names or images were burned. At Abydos, such rites called for a figure of the Seth animal to be drawn in red ink, with his name and the name(s) of who- or whatever else was to be banished written on the figure's chest. The papyrus or wax figures were stabbed, stomped, spit on, speared and otherwise abused before finally being consumed in fire.

The following excerpt from a Middle Kingdom execration formula might serve a more general purpose for the banishment of misfortune and negative energy:

"Every evil word, every evil speech, every evil thought, every evil plot, every evil thing, and every evil dream."

Naming, apotheosis – Hymns and magical chants often named a person's, or thing's, individual parts and identified each one with a particular deity. In the case of spells to cure bites and stings, one can imagine the rhythmic chanting having a potentially soothing or hypnotic effect upon the distressed patient. But the spells had the additional benefit of assigning each part being named with the protection of a god or goddess.

A spell to protect one's house from malevolent ghosts identified the door bolt with Ptah, the windows with Ra as the Great Tomcat (an avatar in which Ra defeats Apophis), and the bed with the "Four Noble Ladies", Isis and Nephthys, Neith and Serket.

Another dramatic example of naming and apotheosis comes from the Metternich Stela, in which Ra heals his feline daughter of a scorpion sting. The original text is quite long - the majority of the stela, which is actually a *cippus*, deals with Isis healing Horus the child - but the major portions of the Ra-and-daughter interlude are excerpted below (updated from Budge's translation in Legends of the Egyptian Gods):

Chapter of Encircling the Cat
(also translated "Casting a Spell on the Cat")

Words to be spoken:

Hail, Ra, come to Your daughter! A scorpion has stung her on a lonely road. Her cry reaches unto the sky and is heard along the roads. The poison has entered her body and circulates through her flesh. She has set her mouth against it, for the poison is in her limbs. Come then, with Your might, Your ferocity and Your red strength, and force it to be hidden before You!

'Lo, the poison has entered all the limbs of this Cat which is under My fingers. Fear not, fear not, My daughter, My perfection, for I have placed Myself near you. I have overthrown the poison which is in all the limbs of this Cat.'

Oh Cat, your head is the head of Ra, Lord of the Two Lands who smites the rebels. Oh Cat, your eyes are the eyes of the Uraeus [*Yarit*], who illluminates the Two Lands and lightens the darkened path. Oh Cat, your nose is the nose of Djehuty, Twice Great, who gives breath to the noses of all people. Oh Cat, your ears are the ears of the Lord of All, who hears the voices of all who call upon Him. Oh Cat, your mouth is the mouth of Atum, Uniter [*Khnum*] of Creation, and He shall deliver you from every poison... Oh Cat, your hands are the hands of the Great and Little Enneads, and They shall deliver your hands from the poison of the mouth of every serpent...

There is no part of you that is without a God or a Goddess who shall overthrow the poison of every male serpent, every female serpent, every scorpion and every reptile which may be in any of your limbs, Oh Cat. Perfect is the *heka* of Ra-Horakhety, Great God, Foremost of the North and South, who says: "Oh evil poison which is in any member of this Cat, come out, issue forth upon the earth!"

Cartomancy - As described above, this technique of divination involved choosing between two or more potsherds, papyrus tickets, or in the case of the Greco-Roman rite described below, palm fronds:

From Greek Magical Papyri XXIV

"Great is the Lady Isis!" Copy of a holy book found in the archive of Hermes [identified with Anubis or Djehuty]: The method is that concerning the 29 letters through with Hermes [Djehuty or Anubis] and Isis, who was seeking Osiris, her brother and husband, (found him).

"Call upon Helios [Ra] and all the gods in the deep [*Duat*] concerning these things for which you want to receive an omen. Take 29 leaves of a male date palm and write on each of the leaves the names of the gods. Pray and then pick them up two by two. Read the last remaining leaf and you will find your omen, how things are, and you will be answered clearly."

Modern *Heka*

As explained in the introduction, practicing *heka* is not quite the same as practicing "Craft" because *heka* cannot be wholly separated from the devotional aspects of Egyptian Paganism in the same manner that "Craft" magick can. By the same token, Kemetic devotional observances often contain elements of *heka*. Two of the examples given below can be incorporated into feast day rituals, such as those in Chapter 7.

Making A *Sa*-Amulet:

This example of protective *heka* adapts a spell from "The Book of the Last Day of the Year", translated by J.F. Borghouts. Its instructional rubric, like most Egyptian spells' rubrics, occurs at the very end and describes the spell as "*A means to save a man from the plague of the year; an enemy will have no power over him*". The actual directions read as follows:

"Words to be said over a piece of fine linen. These gods are to be drawn on it and it is fitted with twelve knots. To offer them bread and beer and burning incense. To be applied to a man's throat."

Therefore, first you will need a piece of fine white fabric. Long and narrow will work best, as you'll be rolling it up and tying knots into it, then making a necklace out of it. Linen is harder to come by these days, so check specialty fabric stores. You'll also need a black marker. "These gods" to be drawn are named in the recitation, but in certain cases are rather obscure. If you have trouble drawing, or can't think of what Shentit or Shesmetet might look like, write down their names instead. To Egyptian thinking, a written name was just as powerful as an image.

As you write or draw, read aloud the following:

"Hail, Sakhmet, Great One, Mistress of the Isheru!
Hail, Shentit, Who sojourns in Busiris!
Hail, Ruler, Ra, Lord of Heaven!
Hail, Shesmetet, Mistress of Punt!
Hail, Horus, Lord of Behdet!
Hail, Sobek, Lord of the Marsh!
Hail, Ir-Isheru!

Hail, Eye of Ra, Mistress of the Two Lands, Ruler of the Isle of Flame!
Hail, Horus of the *Akhu* spirits of Opet!
Hail, He Under His Moringa Tree, Horus, Lord of Shenit!
Hail, Glorious Eye of Horus, Mistress of Wine!
Hail, Khnum, Lord of the House of Thirty!"

When you are finished writing or drawing, perform an offering rite with bread, beer and incense. Read aloud the next part:

"Hail to you gods there! Murderers who stand in waiting upon Sakhmet who have come forth from the Eye of Ra, who bring slaughtering about, who create uproar, who hurry through the land, who shoot their arrows through their mouths, who see from afar! Be on your way, be far from me! Go on, you, I shall not go along with you! You shall have no power over me, for I am Ra who appears in His Eye! I am Atum Who sojourns the Two Lands. I have arisen as Sakhmet, I have arisen as Wadjit, and I will not fall for your slaughtering."

As you tie each knot, read the following:

"I will not fall for your slaughtering, you who are in Pe!
I will not fall for your slaughtering, you who are in Dep!
I will not fall for your slaughtering, you who are in Letopolis!
I will not fall for your slaughtering, you who are in Iunu Heliopolis]!
I will not fall for your slaughtering, you who are in Djedu [Busiris]!
I will not fall for your slaughtering, you who are in Abju [Abydos]!
I will not fall for your slaughtering, you who are in Kher-Aha!
I will not fall for your slaughtering, you who are in heaven!
I will not fall for your slaughtering, you who are in the earth!
I will not fall for your slaughtering, you who are in the meadow!
I will not fall for your slaughtering, you who are in the riverbanks!"

You may notice that the number of statements above totals eleven and not twelve. The twelfth and final knot is probably meant to join the ends of the linen strip and "close" the amulet. As you tie it, read aloud:

"Wadjit is pacified! The attack of those among the wandering demons shall pass over. My *heka* is the protection [*sa*] of my body, so that I am kept whole. Horus, offspring of Sakhmet, put yourself behind my body, so that it is kept whole for life!"

Congratulations! You've made a *sa* amulet for yourself that you can wear. This is an excellent ritual activity for the Epagomenal Days, or *Heriu Diu*, covered in Chapter 7.

A Spell To Dispel Nightmares

The following spell begins as a dialogue between Horus and Isis. You can either use images of Horus and Isis and read both their parts, or get a friend to role-play with you. (This could also be a way to help a friend experiencing nightmare problems.) Read aloud:

"Come to me, my mother Isis! Look, I see something which is far from me, in my own town!"

"Look, my son Horus, come out with what you have seen, so that your delirium will finish and your dream apparitions draw back! A fire will leap out against the thing that frightened you. Look, I have come to see you, so that I may drive out your vexations, that I may annihilate all ailments."

Isis' words, "come out with what you have seen", almost suggests a therapeutic dialogue of what nightmares a person is having, but that can be added at the user's discretion. The person needing assistance from nightmares is then to say:

"Hail to you, good dream! May night be seen as day! May all bad ailments brought about by Seth, son of Nut, be driven out. Victorious is Ra over His enemies, victorious am I over my enemies!"

The rubric calls for a kind of bread and fresh herbs - which kind are not specified - to be soaked in beer and myrrh, then rubbed on the person's face. (Mud mask, anyone?) You might have to improvise the ingredients. Since no one has a recipe for *pesen* bread, try using a sourdough instead. Refer to the herbal section under "Correspondences" for ideas on fresh herbs. The Egyptians also had cilantro and fennel, not listed in the herbal. If mixing them in beer and myrrh is not an option (for example, if you're under legal age to obtain it), you can simply eat the bread and herbs.

Casting Out Negative Influences

For this spell you will need to find a red earthenware pot. The kinds sold in garden sections are inexpensive and work ideally for this purpose. Take a red or black marker and write on the pot:

"Every evil word, every evil speech, every evil thought, every evil plot, every evil fight, every evil disturbance, every evil plan, every evil thing, every evil dream in every evil sleep."

You can add to it specific things that are bothering you, but be extremely cautious; unintended consequences can be nasty! Be specific and avoid listing individuals. When you are done, take the pot someplace where you can smash it to bits and let the pieces become one with the earth, such as a downhill corner or a culvert. No recitations accompany this spell, but for emphasis you can add this banishment originally from an execration of Seth:

"Be gone! You shall not be!
Be gone! Your name shall not be!
Be gone! Your power shall not be!
Be gone! Your *bau* [manifestations] shall not be!"
- *adapted from Siegfried Schott,* *Book of Victory Over Seth*

These three spells are enough to give you a general idea of how Egyptian *heka* operates. Those interested in learning more about *heka* are encouraged to consult the bibliography. Be creative, but cautious, and use the skills you develop wisely.

Hymns to the Notjeru

The hymns below are compiled from a variety of ancient sources and honor deities who figure prominently in major holidays, which will be covered in the next chapter. Sadly for those of us interested in reading them aloud, Egyptian hymns are often not translated in a rhythmic or readable pattern by Egyptologists. Thus, a few liberties have been taken with the source translations in order to produce English versions with some sense of rhythm. If you desire to tweak them further, or rather to match them more closely to the original sources, those are listed for each.

If you happen to be musically inclined, these selections could present a grand opportunity to develop instrumental accompaniment or even sung versions. You could find inspiration or even an audience online; see "Books and Online References" for links to forums, websites and YouTube channels.

Hymn to Ptah:

- *from the Shabaka Stone, Ancient Egyptian Literature vol.I*

Eyes seeing, ears hearing, noses breathing,
All these report to the heart;
It makes all understanding come forth.
Tongue repeats what heart has devised.

Thus were all the gods born,
Atum and his Ennead,
For every word of the god comes about

Through what the heart plans
And the tongue commands.

Thus was Ptah satisfied
After making all things and sacred words.

He gave birth to the gods,
He made Their villages,
He founded Their estates,
Set Them in Their temples,
Ensured Their offerings,
Founded Their shrines,
Made Their bodies as They wished.

Thus the gods entered Their bodies,
Of every wood, stone, and clay,
All things that grow upon Him,
In which They came to be.

Thus were gathered unto Him
All the gods and Their *ka*s,
Contented and united
With the Lord of the Two Lands.

Hymn to Hathor

- *combining New Kingdom love songs and Hathor hymns from Denderah, Ancient Egyptian Literature vols.II and III*

Oh Golden One, come to our song
And feast Your heart on dancing!
Shine upon the festival night,
Take joy in seeing the dances!

chorus:
We praise the Golden Goddess
We worship Her majesty
We exalt the Lady of Heaven
Give chanting to our mistress!

Oh come to the procession of revelry,
To the place where we wander the marsh!
Your rites have been established,
Nothing is left for want!

chorus:
We praise the Golden Goddess
We worship Her majesty
We exalt the Lady of Heaven
Give chanting to our mistress!

How the beauty of Your face shines
As You appear, O come in peace!
We get drunk looking at You,
Beautiful as gold, O Hathor.
May the waters You provide us
Refresh our mouths and cool our hearts.

chorus:
We praise the Golden Goddess
We worship Her majesty
We exalt the Lady of Heaven
Give chanting to our mistress!

Golden One, how good is this song,
Like the song of Horus Himself!
Likewise, see how we dance for You;
Likewise, see how we sing for You!
Give that we may live and prosper!

Hymn to Neith:

- *from* Great Goddesses of Egypt

You are the Mistress of Sais,
Of both masculine and feminine.
Unique Goddess, mysterious and great,
Who came to be in the beginning
And caused everything to come to be.
Mother of Ra, shining in the horizon,
Mysterious One who radiates Her brightness.

Father of fathers and Mother of mothers, the Goddess who came into being was in the midst of Nun, having appeared out of Herself while the land was in twilight. No land had yet come forth and no plant had yet grown. She shone the rays of Her two eyes and dawn came into being. The She said:

"Let this place become land for Me in the midst of Nun, that I might rest upon it."

And this place became land in the midst of Nun, just as She had said. Thus became Iunyt and Sau. Thus She was pleased with this mound, thus Egypt came into being in rejoicing.

Hymn to Sakhmet:

- *from* Great Goddesses of Egypt

Hail to Thee, Lady of Fragrance,
Great Sakhmet, Sovereign Lady.
Oh, Worshipped One,
Serpent upon Her father;
Your rays illumine the Two Lands,
The Two Lands are under Your sway.

Hymn to Min

- *from the stela of Sobek-iry,* Ancient Egyptian Literature vol.I

Adoration to Min, to Horus praise;
He with His arm upraised!
Hail Min in His going forth,
Lofty of Plumes,
Son of Osiris,
Born of Isis.
Great in the Dual Shrines,
Mighty in Ipu,
You of Gebju.
Horus the strong-armed,
Lord of reverence
Who brings pride to silence,
Sovereign of the gods!
Fragrant when He comes from Medja-land,
You of Utent, hail and praise!

Egyptian-Language Hymns

One of the most frequent requests I receive on the Kemetic Independent Channel is for rituals in the original Egyptian language. While an entire service in Egyptian would require years of study and likely prove daunting to even the boldest of Kemetic Reconstructionists, liturgical hymns present a good medium-level challenge for those interested in trying to read and speak ancient Egyptian. Use the pronunciation key below to familiarize yourself with the specific sounds, as they may differ from what you've grown to expect in English. (Remember, George Bernard Shaw observed that British and Americans are "separated by a common language"!) If you find yourself stumped, log onto YouTube and go to the Kemetic Independent Channel; requests are always welcome.

You may also notice that some of the Egyptian words have other vowels in place of the usual 'e', such as *Inodj har-ek* instead of *Inedj her-ek*, as it would appear in most Egyptological sources. Where possible I have compared the Middle Egyptian words, which usually lack vowels, with their matching equivalents in Coptic that include vowel sounds. This helps to distinguish words with different meanings that might otherwise sound the same without restored vowels: such as the Egyptian words for “mother” and “dead person”, both rendered *mut* (or *mwt*) but having variations in Coptic spelling. Adding specific vowel sounds also helps the text to develop a more natural flow for reading aloud.

Practice reading the hymns in a steady, even tempo. If you have a sistrum – and space where you won’t disturb others – try using it to keep rhythm as you recite. Don’t despair if you stumble at first; it takes repetition to learn sound combinations that are not part of our native speech. Keep trying, don’t go too fast, and eventually you will get the hang of it.

Pronunciation Key:

a = 'ah' sound as in 'falling'

e = 'eh' as in 'let'

i = short 'i' as in 'pick'

o = short 'o' as in 'wonder'

u = long 'oo' as in 'super'

Special sounds:

a' = brief 'ah' with a stop, similar to 'uh-oh'

iu = 'ew' as in 'pew'

kh = guttural 'ch' sound, found in Jewish word 'chutzpah'

tj = '-tch' as in 'itch'

Hymn to Ra-Horakhety

(from the papyrus of Nakht - printed in
E. A. Wallis Budge's The Egyptian Book of the Dead)

Inodj har-ek, akh-ti soped, Atum-Horakhety,
Hail to You, One transfigured and sharp, Atum-Horakhety,

iu-ek khaat im akhet net pet, iyau nek im ro en heru nibu.
Who rises in the horizon of heaven, all people rejoice unto You!

Nofer-ti, ronpy teri-ti im Aton im khenu ah
Beautiful One, refreshed in Your time as Aton within the hand

muat-ek Hat-Hor, khaa irek im sut nibet ib nib a'wi en djet.
of Your mother Hathor, You arise
in every place and every heart rejoices.

Iiu-nek Itrety im kes, rdi-sen iyau en uben-ek.
The Dual Shrines pay homage when You come, rejoice when You rise.

Khaaty im akhet net pet, sitet-ek Tawy mafkety.
Arising in the horizon of heaven,
You shed turquoise rays upon the Two Lands.

Ra pu Horakhety, pa hun notjeri,
Ra, who is Horus of the Horizon, the divine child,

uau neheh, tut-su mos-tu djos-ef,
Heir of eternity, Who engendered and birthed Himself,

nisut ta pen, heqa Duat, hir semty Iugeret,
King of this earth, Ruler of Duat, Chief of the Desert Necropolis,

por im mu, setu-su im Nun, ren-su, djoser mos-tu-ef!
emerging from the waters, You drew yourself from Nun,
nursed Yourself, raised yourself!

Notjer ankh, neb merit, ankh her nibu pesed-ek,
Living God, Lord of Love, all people live when You shine,

khaa-ti im Nisut Notjeru!
crowned as King of the Gods!

Ir-en Nut nyny en har-ek, hepet-tu Ma'at er teriu nib.
Nut greets Your face, You embrace Ma'at in all seasons.

Hai-nek imi-khut-ek, dehen-sen har ta im khesfu-ek.
Those in Your following sing Your praise,
touching faces to the ground at Your approach.

Neb pet, neb ta, Nisut Ma'at, neb neheh, heqa djet,
Lord of Heaven, Lord of Earth, King of Ma'at,
Lord of Eternity, Ruler of Everlastingness,

ity notjeru nibu, notjer ankh, iri neheh,
Prince of all the Gods, Living God, Maker of Eternity,

qemem pet semun su im khenu-es!
Creator of Heaven Who establishes what is in it!

Paut notjeru im henu uben-ek,
The Ennead is in jubilation when You rise,

ta im rashut en ma'a sitet-ek.
the earth in joy at seeing Your rays.

Per pat im hai er ma'a noferu-ek ra nib.
The Elders emerge in praise to see Your splendor every day.

Dja-ek hiret ta ra nib s'udja-ti en muat-ek Nut.
You sail above the earth every day, strengthened in Your mother Nut.

Nehemi-ek hiret, ib-ek a'wi.
You traverse what is above, and Your heart gladdens.

Hymn to Amun-Ra

(from the Stela of Suti and Hor -
combined translations of De Buck and Lichtheim)

Inodj har-ek Ra, nofer en ra nib, uben duau an ir-ef a'bu,
Hail to You, Ra, perfect every day, Who rises at dawn without fail,

Khopri uredj im ka't! Setu-ek im har an rekh-tu-es,
Khepri who wearies With labor!
Your rays are upon the face, yet unknown,

Djahm nan su mi ima'u-ek. Pteh-tju neb-ek hau-ek,
Electrum does not match Your splendor.
Self-made You fashioned Your body,

moses iuti mos-tu-ef, wah hir khu-ef, sebeb neheh,
Creator uncreated, Sole One Who traverses eternity,

hiri waut im hehu kher sek-ef. Mi ima'u-ek mi ima-u heret,
Distant One with millions under His care.
Your splendor is like heaven's splendor,

tjehen iun-ek er inem-es. Dja-ek pet, har nib har ma'-ek.
Your color brighter than its hues.
When You cross the sky, all faces see you.

Shem-ek, imun-ti im har sen. Dja-ek tju duau kheret-heru.
When You set, You are hidden from sight.
Daily You give Yourself at dawn,

Rudj seqed-ek kher Hem-ek. Heru ketu hepet-ek wa't,
Safe is Your sailing under Your Majesty.
In a brief day You race a course,

iteru im hehu hefenu. A't heru nib her-ek seb-es hotep-ek,
hundred thousands, millions of miles. Each day is a moment
to You that has passed when You go down.

Kem-en-nek unwaut gereh mitet.
You have completed the night hours likewise,

Gesges-en-ek su en khoper a'bu im ka't-ek.
You have ordered it without pause in Your labor.

Irit nib ma'-sen im-ek, nan kem-sen kheft hotep Hem-ek.
Through You all eyes see, they do nothing when
Your Majesty goes down.

Senhep-ek er uben duau, hadjedjut-ek uba'-es irtu aut.
When You stir to rise at dawn, Your light opens the eyes of the flocks.

Hotep-ek im manu, kher qed-sen mi sekher mut.
When You set in the western mountain, they sleep as if in death.

Inodj har-ek, Aton en heru, qema' tem ir ankh-sen!
Hail to You, Aton of daytime, Creator Who makes all live!

Bik a'ah, sa'b shuty, khoperer sotjes su djos-ef,
Great falcon, brightly plumed, scarab beetle Who raised Himself,

khoper djos-ef, iuti mos-tu-ef,
Who created Himself, uncreated,

Hor semes hir-ib Nut, irer-nef iheh ii en khaa en hotep-ef mitet.
Eldest Horus within Nut, acclaimed in His rising and setting.

neb en qema' sa'tju, Khnum Amun hanmemit,
Creator of the earth's produce, Khnum and Amun of mankind,

itj Tawy em a'ah er nedjes, mut a'khet notjeru romitj,
Who takes the Two Lands from great to small,
beneficent mother of gods and men,

hemu wah-ib a'ah uredj im iry-sen, hu qeni hu aut-ef,
patient craftsman Who toils to make them countless,
brave shepherd who drives His flock,

ib-sen iry ankh-sen, uni, ges, paherer, Khopri tjeni mosut-ef,
their refuge who gives them life, Runner, Racer, Courser,
Khepri distinguished of birth,

setjes nofer-ef im khut en Nut, sehadj Tawy im Aton-ef,
Who raises His beauty in the body of Nut,
Who lightens the Two Lands with His disc,

pauti Tawy ir su djes-ef, ma' iry-ef, neb wah,
Oldest One of the Two Lands Who created Himself,
Who sees what He has made, He alone,

in ra'ah ta'u ra nib im deg khenedu har-es,
Who reaches the ends of the earth every day
in sight of those who tread it,

uben im pet khoperu im Ra!
rising in the sky formed as Ra!

Ir-ef teru im a'bdu heh mer-ef, qebeb mer-ef.
He makes seasons within months, heat as
He wishes, cold as He wishes.

Dji-ef bedesh hau ineq-ef sen.
He makes bodies slack, He gathers them.

Ta nib im hetjet en uben-ef ra nib.
Every land rejoices in His rising every day.

Hymn to Osiris

(from the Stela of Amunmose, in Budge's Legends of the Egyptian Gods
and Lichtheim's *Ancient Egyptian Literature vol.II*)

Inodj har-ek Osir, neb neheh, nisut notjeru,
Praise to You, Osiris, Lord of Eternity, King of the Gods,

asha' ranu, djoser khoperu, seshta iru im pir!
of many names, of holy forms, of secret rites in temples!

Shopses ka pu khenty Djadu, ur geret im Sakhem,
This noble *ka* at the fore of Djedu, great also in Sekhem,

neb hekenu im Andjety, khenty djefa im Iunu,
lord of praise in Andjety, foremost of offerings in Iunu,

neb sekhau im Ma'aty, ba seshta, neb kereret,
Lord of memory in *Ma'aty*, secret *ba*, lord of the cavern,

djoser im Ineb-hadj, ba Ra djet-ef djos-ef,
holy in White-Walls, *ba* of Ra of His very body,

hotep im Henes, monekh henu im narit,
at rest in Henes, excellent of praise in the *narit*-tree

khoper-es tjesit ba-ef. Neb hat a'ah im Khemnu,
that grew to raise His *ba*. Lord of the Great Shrine in Khemnu,

a'ah niru im Shas-hotep, neb neheh, khenty Abju
great of terror in Shas-hotep, Lord of Eternity, foremost of Abydos

hir wai sut-ef im Ta-Djoser.
in His distant place of the Sacred Land.

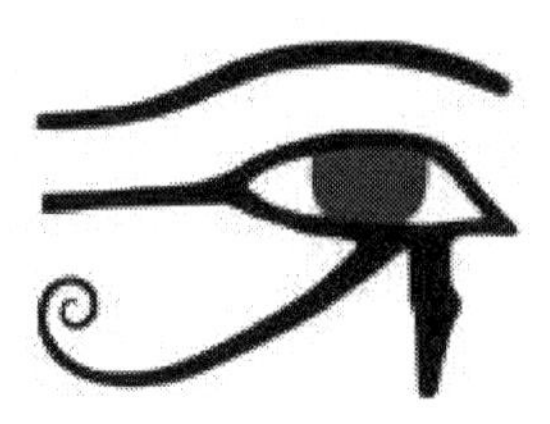

A Year of Kemetic Observance

A young Egyptologist could probably spend their entire career just studying Egyptian festivals. No two areas observed the same calendar, and even national holidays varied from one region to another and from one period of time to the next. Surviving records are rich in some details, sparse in others. Scholars have a plethora of information about some holidays, such as the Feasts of the Valley and the Beautiful Reunion, which were observed in temples that remained well-preserved. Other festivals, such as the Feasts of Makhir and Apip, left few references and are now frustratingly obscure.

As an Egyptian Pagan, however, you have the advantage of being allowed to follow your intuition. On more than one occasion I have written and performed a ritual using a "best guess" when I could not find enough published research as a starting point. The resulting service was not only enjoyed by everyone who participated, but also confirmed to be in the correct spirit when I found more historical resources later. Read and study where you can, but don't be afraid to let your instinct guide you when you've reached the limits of available scholarship.

The major holidays listed here are presented in a solitary format, but can be adapted for use as a group ritual. I encourage all readers, Tameran Wiccan, Kemetic Reconstructionist or other, to take a "plug-and-play" approach using components that best fit your needs. Even the most elaborate rituals can still be broken down into component sections or acts. Once you become familiar with the basic forms, you can combine, rearrange or build around them as necessary.

Just bear in mind that whether you are enacting a solitary ritual or a group feast, you are *performing*. Make sure you have a "script" of your personalized ritual, and give yourself time to read over it and practice beforehand. If you are in a group, make sure that other participants know and understand their parts as well. Of course, if you stumble over a line or a section of the rite it won't mean the end of the world (contrary to fears even some ancient Egyptians had). But a little practice can potentially help you save face. One coven whose open Sabbats I used to attend printed out their Mabon ritual barely an hour before time for circle a few years ago. They mixed up their elements and directions, only discovering the error in mid-quarter call - all while videotaping the ritual!

Reviewing Egyptian Months and Seasons

Ancient Egypt was an agrarian society, but their seasons did not match what we know today. The year began with the Nile floods and *Akhet*, or Inundation, which began in mid- to late-July and lasted four months. After the floodwaters receded, planting began and the first signs of sprouting grain heralded *Peret* (also rendered *Proyet*), or "Emergence". This season began in mid-November, and actually corresponds to winter in much of the Northern Hemisphere. Egyptian harvest time took place at the start or summer, or *Shomu*, beginning in March. After four months of summer, the cycle began again.

Months were generally numbered, such as Akhet I, Peret I, Shomu I, and so on. Less often months were referred to by names, which referred to the major feast that took place at the end of that month. So, for example, the month of Hat-Hor (Akhet III) was so named for the "Sailing of Hathor" feast which took place at the end of the month.

Use the tables below to find Egyptian months and holidays with their modern correspondences. Notice that some month names changed from the Middle to the New Kingdom eras; this provides just one more illustration of how Egyptian liturgical calendars evolved over time. As you adapt holidays and dates to your own group or personal practice, you will be simply continuing that tradition.

Egyptian Civil Calendar With Modern Dates			
Middle Kingdom Month Names	**New Kingdom Month Names**	**Greek Month Names**	**Modern Dates**
Akhet - Season of Inundation			
Tekhy	Djehutet	Thoth	July 18 - August 16
Menhet	Pa'en-Opet	Paopi	Aug. 17 - Sept. 15
Hat-Hor	Hat-Hor	Hathor	Sept. 16 - Oct. 16
Ka-Her-Ka	Ka-Her-Ka	Khoiakh	Oct. 17 - Nov. 14
Peret - Season of Emergence			
Saf-Bedhet	Ta-ibet	Tybi	Nov. 15 - Dec. 15
Rekh-ur	Makhir	Mechir	Dec. 16 - Jan. 13
Rekh-nedjes	Pa'en-Amunhotepu	Jan. 14 - Feb. 12	Panemot
Rennutet	Pa'en-Rennutet	Parmuti	Feb. 13 - March 15
Shomu - Season of Summer			
Khonsu	Pa-Khonsu	Pachons	March 16 - April 13
Henet-Hetj	Pa'en-Inet	Payni	April 14 - May 13
Ipet-Hemet	Apip	Epipi	May 14 - June 12
Up-Ronpet	Mosu-Ra	Mesore	June 13 - July 12
Days Upon the Year: July 13 - 17			

Use the table above to compare Egyptian months with their modern dates. The Greek month names are commonly used in Isian and Tameran systems.

Egyptian Liturgical Calendar

Festival or Observance	Original Egyptian Date	Modern Date or Holiday	Corresponding Wiccan Sabbat
Days Upon the Year	Intercalary Days	July 13 - 17	(none)
Upet Ronpet	1 Djehutet	July 18	Lammas (Aug. 1)
Wagy-Djehutet	17-19 Djehutet	August 3-5	Lammas
Opet Festival	15-26 Pa'en-Opet	Aug. 31 – Sept.10	Mabon (Sept. 21)
Sailing of Hathor	30 Hat-Hor	October 16	(none)
Feast of Sokar/ Khoiakh Mysteries	17-30 Ka-Her-Ka	Oct. 27 - Nov. 14	Samhain (Oct. 31)
Hab Sed/ Feast of NehebKau Coronation of the Sacred Falcon	1 Ta'ib	November 15	(none)
Sailing of Mut	30 Ta'ib	December 14	Yule (Dec. 21)
Feast of Victory	21-25 Makhir	January 4	Yule
Feast of Lifting the Sky	30 Makhir	January 13	Yule, Imbolc (Feb. 1)
Feast of Min/ Rennutet/ Khnum	30 Pa-Khonsu	April 13	Ostara (March 21)
Feast of the Valley	15 Pa'en-Inet	April 28	Beltane (May 1)
Feast of the Reunion	7 Apip (approx.)	May 20	Beltane, Litha (June 21)
Feast of Neith	13 Apip	May 27	Litha
Feast of Apip	30 Apip	June 12	(none)
Day of Mosyt	30 Mosu-Ra	July 12	(none)

Use this table to find major Egyptian feast days, and their closest Wiccan Sabbat equivalents (if any).

The Festivals

Epagomenal Days - *Heru Diu Her Ronpet*

Historical background: Following the end of one civil calendar year and preceding the New Year were the Five Epagomenal Days, or the "Five Days Upon the Year" - called the *Heriu Diu* (the "Five Days") for short. Considered the birth days of the five gods Osiris, Horus, Seth, Isis and Nephthys, the Days Upon the Year were seen as a liminal period when cyclical time, *neheh*, stopped briefly and linear time, *djet*, took over.

Because of the potentially precarious state of the universe during this transitional period, Egyptians focused on protective rites for their observances. *Sehotep Sakhmet* ("Placation of Sakhmet") litanies were read to invoke Sakhmet's protection during the transitional period, and people drew protective charms of deities and magical figures onto white linen to wear around their necks. In temples, torches were kept lit to drive away evil forces. The birthday of Seth was considered an especially precarious time, and wherever possible people avoided conducting transactions or other important business on that day.

During the Late Period, protective rituals became increasingly more complex and paranoid, perhaps reflecting the political climate of the day. Papyrus records detail private rites performed by priests within the *Per Ankh*, or scriptorium, of temples in order to protect and renew the king. So dangerous were these rites that for most of them a stand-in actually took the king's place! The substitute 'king' was covered with protective amulets and slept on a bed that had a protective ring of sand on the floor around it, all the while keeping a seal of royal inheritance with him. Subsequent rites involved live falcons, vultures and geese, birds associated with gods of kingship, and anointing the king with an actual falcon's tear to symbolize the Eye of Horus.

Other rites meant to allow Ra and Osiris to merge, again referring to the eternally renewing *neheh* aspect of time embodied by Ra, and the eternally same *djet* aspect embodied in Osiris. These rituals called for the replacement of a special "mummy" effigy of Osiris housed in a pine box within the *Per Ankh*. The point at which one form of Osiris was taken out of the coffin so another could be placed inside was seen as a critically dangerous point, and elaborate protective rites were done throughout the entire operation to ensure a safe transition.

For the average Egyptian, the *Heriu Diu* were probably a time of much anticipation and wishes for good luck in the coming year, just as the time before New Year's is today in most modern cultures.

Modern observance: If one of your patron deities is one of the five born during the Days On the Year, take the opportunity to celebrate them on that day. Find a tall candle to light each evening for prayer, reflection or offerings. If you have goals or requests for the upcoming year, include those in your prayers. Reflect on what things you want to be rid of this year. Use the Invocation to Sakhmet in prayers for good fortune, protection and blessing. If you practice *heka*, try making a *Heriu Diu* or New Year's amulet for yourself or your friends.

You will need: Milk, water, food offerings, wine; tall white candles. The glass "jar"-type commonly found in supermarkets or Mexican grocery stores work especially well.

Altar setup: It's not likely that you'll have icons of all five deities celebrated during the Epagomenal Days, but for those whom you do, let Them take center stage on Their appropriate day. Sakhmet can also take prominence, particularly for recitals of Her litany. Make a space on your altar for your holiday candle; while burning it constantly presents a fire hazard, you can leave it lit for as long as you're in that area. (One alternative would be to use battery-powered electric candles and leave them lit for the lifespan of the batteries.) Leave room in the front of the altar space for offerings and flowers; if making amulets, prepare a clean and ritually purified workspace near your altar as well. If you can sprinkle sand or natron at the perimeters, do so. If this is not an option - for example, if you'd end up vacuuming sand or salt out of your carpet! - make four natron bundles and place them at the cardinal points.

(In preparation, perform the necessary purifications for yourself and your altar space.)

Candle Rite - As you light your candle(s), say:

"Come in peace, bright Eye of Horus, come in peace. Receive the light.
The Eye of Horus shines, like Ra in the twin Horizons, and evil hides before it. Receive the light.
The Eye of Horus destroys the enemies of Ra in all of their abodes. Receive the light.
The Eye of Horus comes, and I am purified with it. Receive the light."

- *from the Daily Rite of Amun-Ra, Karnak, and Book of the Dead chapter 137B*

Opening Invocation – Ring your sistrum. If part of a group, everyone recites:

"Great Ennead of the gods who are in Iunu (yoo-NOO)!
Ra, in Your appearance at the First Time;
Ra's Twins, Shu and Tefnut;
Geb and Nut, Lord of Earth and Lady of Heaven;
Osiris [Osir], Isis [Iset], Set and Nephthys (NEF-tis) [Nebet-Hat];
Turn Your faces toward us!
Behold what is in our innermost;
Our hearts are straight, our hearts are open,
No darkness is in our hearts!"

- *adapted from Osiris hymn of Amunmose and hymn to Hathor in Denderah, Ancient Egyptian Literature vols. II and III*

Invocations to the Deities – The fourfold invocations for each deity of the Epagomenal Days are given; use the specific invocation for each day. You can read either the Egyptian-language version or the English one, whichever you feel most comfortable pronouncing. (See "Books and Online Resources" for more information.) If observing as a group, try having one person read the Egyptian portion and the other participants respond in English, or take turns.

(ring sistrum)

Day One: Osiris

Iiu im hotep, Osir, neb Abju.
- Come in peace, Osiris, Lord of Abydos.

Iiu im hotep, Osir, neb neheh.
- Come in peace, Osiris, Lord of Eternal Renewal.

Iiu im hotep, Osir, Khenti-Amentiu.
- Come in peace, Osiris, Foremost of the Westerners.

Iiu im hotep, Osir, Un-en-nofer.
- Come in peace, Osiris, the Beatified.

Day Two: Horus

Iiu im hotep, Horu, Ba Iabty.
- Come in peace, Horus, Ba of the East.

Iiu im hotep, Horu, Nedj-Her-It-ef.
- Come in peace, Horus, Defender of His Father.

Iiu im hotep, Horu, notjer a'ah.
- Come in peace, Horus, Greatest God.

Iiu im hotep, Horu, neb pet.
- Come in peace, Horus, Lord of the Sky.

Day Three: Seth

Iiu im hotep, Set, neb Nubet.
- Come in peace, Set, Lord of Ombos.

Iiu im hotep, Set, neb deshret.
- Come in peace, Set, Lord of the desert.

Iiu im hotep, Set, a'ah pehty.
- Come in peace, Set, Greatest of Strength.

Iiu im hotep, Set, sa Nut.
- Come in peace, Son of Nut.

Day Four: Isis
Iiu im hotep, Iset, Uret Hekau.
- Come in peace, Isis, Great of Magic.
Iiu im hotep, Iset, Mut Notjer.
- Come in peace, Isis, Mother of the God.
Iiu im hotep, Iset, notjerit a'ah.
- Come in peace, Isis, Greatest Goddess.
Iiu im hotep, Iset, nebet pet.
- Come in peace, Isis, Mistress of the Sky.

Day Five: Nephthys
Iiu im hotep, Nebet-hat, nebet Notjeru.
- Come in peace, Nephthys, Mistress of the Gods.
Iiu im hotep, Nebet-hat, nebet ankh.
- Come in peace, Nephthys, Mistress of Life.
Iiu im hotep, Nebet-hat, notjerit a'ah.
- Come in peace, Nephthys, Greatest Goddess.
Iiu im hotep, Nebet-hat, nebet pet.
- Come in peace, Nephthys, Mistress of the Sky.

Offering Rite:
Water: "Take these, Your cool waters that are the Inundation."
Milk: "Milk, milk, may You taste it in Your shrine."
Incense: "I give You incense, I give You incense, great of purity."
Food: "Take this, Your bread, on which gods live."

Presentation of Offerings: "Turn Yourself to these, Your offerings; receive them from me."

Recitation of sacred texts - These are often specific to the festival observance. During the Epagomenal Days you can read from the Litany of Sakhmet given below, the Hymn to Osiris from Chapter 6 on His birthday, or even Chapter 130 of the Book of the Dead ("For Making a Spirit Worthy on the Birthday of Osiris"). If you've written your own hymn or devotional, now is the perfect time to read it.

Invocation to Sakhmet Against the Seven Arrows of the Year:

1) Hail, Sakhmet, Who presides over the land, Lady of Flourishing, Generous One, Sakhmet who protects the Two Lands! Come to us who are under Your sway! Save us, protect us, and preserve us from the First Arrow of the Year!

2) Hail, Sakhmet, oh Curl, oh Hidden Lady, Wadjit the Great! Come to us who are under Your sway! Save us, protect us, and preserve us from the Second Arrow of the Year!

3) Hail, Sakhmet, who moves in light, who terrifies the gods with Her massacre! Come to us who are under Your sway! Save us, protect us, and preserve us from the Third Arrow of the Year!

4) Hail, Sakhmet, who guides mankind, Lady of the Dual Shores, Mistress of humanity! Come to us who are under Your sway! Save us, protect us, and preserve us from the Fourth Arrow of the Year!

5) Hail, Sakhmet, Great Shining One, Foremost in the Mansion of Flame *(Per Neser)*, Who terrorizes the Two Lands with fear! Come to us who are under Your sway! Save us, protect us, and preserve us from the Fifth Arrow of the Year!

6) Hail, Sakhmet, who loves Ma'at and hates *isfet*, Lady of the people! Come to us who are under Your sway! Save us, protect us, and preserve us from the Sixth Arrow of the Year!

7) Hail, Sakhmet, Uraeus who opens the acacia, Great and Sovereign One! Come to us who are under Your sway! Save us, protect us, and preserve us from the Seventh Arrow of the Year!

- *adapted from Richard Reidy's translation from the French from Sekhmet et la Protection du Monde by Phillippe Germond*

(ring sistrum)

Ritual Action: These are the holiday-specific activities, which may be either preceded or followed by readings and hymns. For the Epagomenal Days, you could try making a protective *sa*-amulet, as described in Chapter 5; perform an execration of negativity, also covered under "Modern *Heka*"; or make an Osiris "mummy" and place it in a special box.

Prayer: This can be your time for silent prayer, meditation, and so on. Let the energy you've built up slowly release itself. When you're ready, ring your sistrum, or other instrument if you have one. Or you can improvise; some Buddhists use the distinctive sound of prayer beads rubbed together, for example, to indicate a stopping point in chanting or prayer.

Closing Invocation:
Great Ennead of the gods in Iunu!
Ra, in Your appearance at the First Time;
Ra's Twins, Shu and Tefnut;
Geb and Nut, Lord of Earth and Lady of Heaven;
Osiris [Osir], Isis [Iset], Set and Nephthys [Nebet-Hat];
I thank You, and wish You well!
Remember me, be where You like, and come again in kindness!
Seneb-ti!
- *inspired from Osiris hymn of Amunmose*

In-un-Ma'a [Truly it Is]

End of Rite

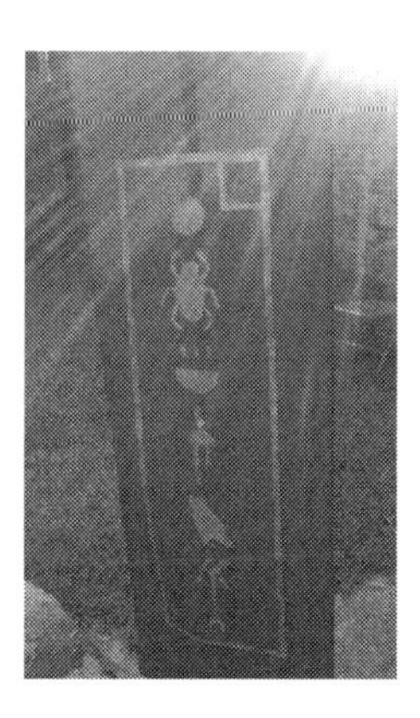

New Year's Day - *Upet Ronpet (Wep Ronpet)*

Historical background: The apotropaic rites of the Days Upon the Year culminated in the celebration of *Upet Ronpet*, literally the "Opening of the Year". A special torch was lit in temples and a teapot-shaped ritual vessel, called a *nemset* jar, was presented in offering to the gods. Torches continued to be burned to chase away evil, and *Sehotep Sakhmet* litanies continued to be read to protect the king and the cosmos in general. Among those hymns was probably a litany addressing the "Seven Arrows of Sakhmet", invoking Sakhmet's protection against the plagues and demons who were under her command as the "Arrows of the Year".

In state rituals, Execration Texts were read and enemies of the state were destroyed in effigy (and possibly sometimes in reality, as evidenced by a mutilated skeleton found amongst ritual deposits at the Mergissa outpost in Nubia). The arch-fiend Apophis was also destroyed in effigy, to commemorate the establishment of order over chaos. Records from the reign of Thutmose III also refer to a mock combat and a procession performed on water. During the Middle Kingdom, some kings chose to celebrate their coronation on New Year's Day. Kings of later periods frequently chose to renew or commemorate their coronation during New Year's, which was referred to in later times as *Mosut Ra-Horakhety*, "Birth of Ra-Horakhety". In the New Kingdom, elite officials often gave their sovereigns gifts that connoted solar themes; during the Late Period, the gift-giving practice extended to the general populace. Items that had once been New Year's gifts, such as jewelry and other personal effects, have been found bearing the inscription *Upet Ronpet Nofrit*, or "Happy New Year".

Other common rituals included throwing ink into the river, symbolizing the efflux from Osiris' body that the ancient Egyptians considered a source of the Nile floodwaters. (This may have formed the antecedent to modern Egyptians' custom of throwing flowers into the Nile for *Wafaa al-Nil*, the Nile Festival.) People also performed rites of self-purification and painted their eyes with green eyepaint, suggesting lushness and renewal.

At Hathor's temple in Denderah, New Year's was a time to pay particular tribute to all goddesses as well as to Ra. Icon statues of the temple deities were taken into special courts to be placed in sunlight, and both Horus and Hathor were thought to merge with Ra and his sunrays. At Edfu, a possible wrap-up to the New Year's festivities was a water procession on the temple lake that took place on the eighth day of the month, called the *Pa-Shemet en Horu* or "Going Forth of Horus".

Modern observance: Some Kemetics today celebrate *Wep Ronpet* in early August, to coincide with the modern heliacal rising of Sirius; others observe it in mid-July. For either date, the meaning remains the same. The "Opening of the Year" marks a time for new beginnings, fresh starts, and (hopefully) opportunities for greater fortune - be they material or spiritual. This religious New Year's date occurs in the middle of our modern civil calendar, offering a possible reference point to reflect on how the secular year has been going so far. Did your January resolutions fade out sometime in March? Make an Egyptian New Year's Resolution. Give a friend that perfect gift you'd been saving for the right opportunity; depending on how familiar they are with your beliefs, you can call it an *Upet Ronpet* gift, or just "Christmas in July". Don't limit your celebration to just the ritual aspect. *Upet Ronpet Nofrit* - Happy New Year!

You will need: Milk, water, food (bread specifically); a ritual adze or athame; a black or dark-colored cup and a white cup; ritual oil for anointing; a wand, scepter or sistrum. Draw and cut out green paper snakes - they don't have to be artistic, just wide enough to write on - beforehand and make sure you have a way to burn them safely. An optional supply is beer and red food coloring; if you have to stick with non-alcoholic choices, an alternative our local circle has used is to put red food coloring in some milk.

Altar setup: Central to the arrangements for *Upet Ronpet* is an image of Ra. In lieu of an icon statue, a model obelisk or pyramid placed on a small decorated box or platform can serve beautifully as a *benben* stone. A scarab can also serve to represent Ra's aspect as Khepri. Arrange your other icons around the representation of Ra. Place your ritual tools and offering area in front of the assembled icons. The New Year's observance is best done outdoors, to take advantage of sunlight; it will also allow more safe options for ritually burning paper Apophis snakes.

Upet Ronpet Ritual

(In preparation, perform the necessary purifications for yourself and your altar space.)

Candle Rite - As you light your candle(s), say:

"Come in peace, bright Eye of Horus, come in peace.
Receive the light.
The Eye of Horus shines, like Ra in the twin Horizons, and evil hides before it. Receive the light.
The Eye of Horus destroys the enemies of Ra in all of their abodes. Receive the light.
The Eye of Horus comes, and I am purified with it.
Receive the light."

- from the Daily Rite of Amun-Ra, Karnak, and Book of the Dead chapter 137B

Opening Invocation – Ring your sistrum. If part of a group, everyone recites:

"Great Ennead of the gods who are in Iunu (yoo-NOO)!
Ra, in Your appearance at the First Time;
Ra's Twins, Shu and Tefnut;
Geb and Nut, Lord of Earth and Lady of Heaven;
Osiris [Osir], Isis [Iset], Set and Nephthys [Nebet-Hat];
Turn Your faces toward us!
Behold what is in our innermost;
Our hearts are straight, our hearts are open,
No darkness is in our hearts!"

- *adapted from Osiris hymn of Amunmose and hymn to Hathor in Denderah,* *<u>Ancient Egyptian Literature vols. II and III</u>*

Invocation to Ra: You can read either the Egyptian-language version or the English one, whichever you feel most comfortable pronouncing. *(ring sistrum)*

Iu im hotep Ra, neb Pesdjet.
– Come in peace, Ra, Lord of the Nine.
Iu im hotep Ra, wa en Nun.
– Come in peace, Ra, Unique One of Nun.
Iu im hotep Ra, neb ankh.
– Come in peace, Ra, Lord of Life.
Iu im hotep Ra, neb meri.
– Come in peace, Ra, Lord of Love.

Recitation of sacred texts - From Spell 1130 of the Coffin Texts, also called "The Monologue of the Creator":

Words spoken by Ra:

"Hail in peace! I repeat to you the good deeds which my own heart did for me from within the serpent's coil, in order to silence strife. I did four good deeds within the *akhet*:

I made the four winds, that every man might breathe in his time. This is one of the deeds.

I made the Inundation, that the humble might benefit by it like the great. This is one of the deeds.

I made every man like his fellow, and I did not command that they do wrong. It is their hearts that disobey what I have said. This is one of the deeds.

I made that their hearts are not disposed to forget the West, in order that sacred offerings be made to the gods. This is one of the deeds.

I have created the gods from my sweat, and the people from the tears of my eye."
(ring sistrum)

Ritual Action - For Upet Ronpet, one focus is on "renewing" icons of the gods under the life-giving rays of Ra's sunlight with a Mouth-Opening ceremony. Two others are the ritual execration of A'apep, or Apophis, and the Appeasement of Sakhmet.

Opening of the Mouth:
Libation: Take these, Your cool waters that are the Inundation, that they may cool Your heart. (*offer water*) Come, __________, you have been invoked. *Repeat three times*: Come, you have been invoked.

Incense: I give you incense, I give you incense, great of purity. Let its scent reach you and purify you. (*offer incense*)

Cleansing the Mouth: This is your natron of Horus, this is your natron of Seth. This is your own natron among the gods. You are purified with it. (*offer natron*) Your mouth is clean as a calf's on the day it is born.

Milk, milk that parts your mouth, may you taste it in your shrines. That of Horus, that of Seth, that of the two gods reconciled, milk. (*pour milk into saucer*)

Opening the mouth and eyes: I have fixed your jaws spread for you. (*touch each statue's face with striker*) Let me part your mouth for you.

Here are your two eyes, black and white; lift them to your face, and illuminate it. (*lift black and white cups*)

Anointing: Ointment, ointment, from the forehead of Ra; I shall put it on you and it shall transfigure you. (*anoint statues with oil*)

Offering and reversion: At peace for you is Ra in the sky. Peace be given for you, peace be what you see, peace be what you hear, peace be before you, peace be behind you, peace be your lot. (*offer bread*)

Ra, may your dawn be for these gods. As every good and pure offering is for you, so let it be for them. (*sweep over offerings with scepter*)

Overthrowing A'apep (Apophis)
Write down negative things which you wish to be rid of for the new year on green paper "A'apep" snakes and ceremonially burn them. For a ritual reading to accompany the activity, use this section from the Papyrus Bremner-Rhind. It would be excellent read aloud as the paper 'snakes' burn:

The Book of Knowing the Forms of Ra, and of Overthrowing A'apep.

"The Lord of All, after having come into being, says: "I am He who came into being as Khepri. When I came into being, the beings came into being, all the beings came into being after I became. Numerous are those who became, who came out of my mouth, before heaven ever existed, nor earth came into being, nor the worms, nor snakes were created in this place. I being in weariness, was bound to them in Nun. I found no place to stand. I thought in my heart, I planned in myself, I made all forms being alone, before I ejected Shu, before I spat out Tefnut, before any other who was in me had become. Then I planned in my own heart, and many forms of being came into being as forms of children, as forms of their children. I conceived by my hand, I united myself with my hand, I poured out of my own mouth. I ejected Shu, I spat out Tefnut. It was my father Nun who brought them up, and my eye followed them, while they became far from me. After having become one god, there were now three gods in me. When I came into being in this land, Shu and Tefnut jubilated in Nun in which they were. Then they brought with them my Eye. After I had joined together my members, I wept over them, and men came into being out of the tears which came out of my eyes. Then She [the Eye] became enraged after She came back and found that I had placed another in Her place, that She had been replaced by the Brilliant One. The I found a higher place for Her on my brow, and when She began to rule over the whole land her fury fell down on the flowering and I replaced what She had ravished. I came out of the flowering, I created all snakes, and all that came into being with them. Shu and Tefnut produced Geb and Nut; Geb and Nut produced out of a single body Osiris, Horus the Eyeless One, Seth, Isis and Nephthys, one after the other among them. Their children are numerous in this land. They invoke My name, They overthrow Their enemies, and They make *heka* for the overthrowing of A'apep, over whose hands and arms Aker keeps guard. His hands and arms shall not exist, his feet and legs shall not exist, and he is chained in one place while Ra inflicts upon him the blows which are decreed for him. He is thrown upon his accursed back, his face is split for the evil he has done, and he shall remain upon his accursed back."

- from R.O. Faulkner's translation, combined with Budge's translation in Legends of the Egyptian Gods

Sehotep Sakhmet Hymn – You can read the Sakhmet Litany from the *Heriu Diu* rites, or use the Hymn to Sakhmet from Chapter 6, or a combination of both.
(ring sistrum)

Prayer: This can be your time for silent prayer, meditation or reflection. Breathe deeply, exhale, and let the energy you've built up slowly release itself.

Closing Invocation: *(ring sistrum)*

"Great Ennead of the gods in Iunu!
Ra, in Your appearance at the First Time;
Ra's Twins, Shu and Tefnut;
Geb and Nut, Lord of Earth and Lady of Heaven;
Osiris [Osir], Isis [Iset], Set and Nephthys [Nebet-Hat];
I thank You, and wish You well!
Remember me, be where You like, and come again in kindness!
Seneb-ti!"

- *inspired from Osiris hymn of Amunmose*

To conclude the rite, say: "*In-un-Ma'a*" [Truly it Is]

End of Rite

A cauldron is the ideal place to burn effigies of Apophis, as seen here. Author's photo.

The *Wagy*, *Djehutet* and *Tekhy* (Drunkenness) Festivals

Historical background: An ancient holiday, the *Wagy* (or *Wag*) Feast dates back to the Old Kingdom. It commemorated Osiris sailing to Abydos and anticipated the resurrecting powers of the Inundation upon the fields. Other references suggest it was considered the jubilee of Osiris. Offerings were made to the deceased and to "Osiris, Lord of Wine in the *Wagy* Festival". The *Wagy*, translated as "Supply", Feast is commonly mentioned in funeral stelae in which the deceased ask to be given food and drink from the altar of Osiris. Spells from the Coffin texts refer to pouring water for the deceased during the *Wagy*, which was likely done in stone "*Nun*" basins found in tomb chapels. The New Kingdom stela of Suti and Hor also mentions garlands, which may have been included in the offerings. An important part of the observance was the "Eve of *Wagy*", and references in texts suggest that torches were lit and carried in a procession for the event.

Greco-Roman texts from Denderah indicate that the Feast of Drunkenness of Hathor was celebrated the day after the *Wagy* Feast. As Hathor-Tefnut, she had to be enticed back to Egypt and propitiated with dancing, music and wine. Much more obscure are the references to a festival of *Tekhy*, or Drunkenness, going back to the Middle Kingdom. Some place this feast on the day after *Djehutet*, but later references place it around the Sailing of Hathor roughly two months later. *Tekhy* refers to Ra's solar Eye, as Hathor or other goddesses, returning from her rampage in the desert after being placated with red-stained beer.

Elsewhere the 19th of Akhet I was fixed as the Feast of Thoth, or *Djehutet*. Honoring Djehuty (Thoth) as "Lord of Hermopolis" and "True Scribe of the Ennead", worshipers honored him with offerings of water-bowls, reed pens and writing palettes. By the Roman era, Plutarch observed that honey, figs and sweets were offered to Djehuty amid chants of "A sweet thing is truth." In one version of the Distant Goddess myth, Djehuty must find her and convince her to return. The Feast of Djehuty may have celebrated his wisdom as the god who brought back the Eye of Ra.

Modern observance: The *Wagy* feast provides an excellent opportunity to remember loved ones with their favorite foods, as well as to honor Osiris and Anubis. The following day, celebrate Djehuty as lord of writing, creativity and education - increasingly popular among the Internet generation, one of His further domains may well be computers! Don't be afraid to request His blessings on your WACOM pen or favorite "smart" device.

If you happen to have a group to celebrate with that is over the legal drinking age, you might also consider a Feast of Drunkenness. But make sure that everyone has a place to stay until well after the festivities are over; drink responsibly, and don't let anyone drive home intoxicated.

You will need: For Day One, you'll need wine and white bread. Day Two will require natron, wine, a white loaf, and food offerings for *akhu* (deceased loved ones) you wish to honor. You may want to keep a list of your honored *akhu* handy. For water offerings, pick out a blue saucer or bowl to serve as a *Nun* basin for the *akhu*, symbolizing renewing life.

Day Three will involve natron, honey and sweets, a writing tool to offer Djehuty, and any tools such as pens, your computer mouse or pen tablet, etc., of your own that you wish to bless.

Altar setup: For Day One, central to the altar will be an icon of Osiris. Day Two will feature Osiris and Anubis. If you're artistically inclined, try making an *imiut* emblem (see photos) to place at one side of your altar. Day Three is dedicated to Djehuty (Thoth). Leave space in front of Djehuty's image for offerings of sweets, and for your writing implements to be blessed. Make sure they aren't too close to candles, oils or other possible sources of damage.

Wagy-Djehutet Rites

Day One: Eve of Wagy

(The Eve of Wagy is a shorter ritual. In preparation, perform the necessary purifications for yourself and your altar space.)

Candle Rite - As you light your candle(s), say:

"Come in peace, bright Eye of Horus, come in peace.
Receive the light.
The Eye of Horus shines, like Ra in the twin Horizons, and evil hides before it. Receive the light.
The Eye of Horus destroys the enemies of Ra in all of their abodes. Receive the light.
The Eye of Horus comes, and I am purified with it.
Receive the light."

- *from the Daily Rite of Amun-Ra, Karnak, and Book of the Dead chapter 137B*

Invocation: *(ring sistrum)*

Iiu im hotep, Osir, neb Abju.
- Come in peace, Osiris, Lord of Abydos.

Iiu im hotep, Osir, neb Djedu.
- Come in peace, Osiris, Lord of Busiris.

Iiu im hotep, Osir, Khenti-Amentiu.
- Come in peace, Osiris, Foremost of the Westerners.

Iiu im hotep, Osir, Un-en-Nefer.
- Come in peace, Osiris, the Beatified.

Offering Rite:

Water: "Take these, Your cool waters that are the Inundation."
Milk: "Milk, milk, may You taste it in Your shrine."
Incense: "I give You incense, I give You incense, great of purity."
Food: "Take this, Your white loaf, on which gods live."
Wine: "Receive this, oh Osir, Your wine on the Eve of Wagy."

(ring sistrum)

Presentation: Turn Yourself to these, Your offerings, oh Osir; and share them with these beloved *Akhu* who are with You in *Duat*:

Voice Offering: You can use the Egyptian or English version.

Peret kheru, ta, heneket, kha khau, apdu, senotjer, merhat, khut nebet nofret wabet ankhet notjer im, en kau en... [read from your list of loved ones, or name them in turn]*...ma'a-kheru her notjer a'ah.*

"A voice offering of bread, beer, a thousand of beef and poultry, incense and oil, and all good and pure things on which a god lives, for the *ka*s of _______, true of voice before the Great God."

(ring sistrum)

"Be at peace, Osir; be at peace, beloved spirits. Peace be given for you, peace be what you see, peace be what you hear, peace be before you, peace be behind you, peace be your lot."
(ring sistrum)

In-un-Ma'a [Truly it Is]

Day Two: Feast of Wagy

(In preparation, perform the necessary purifications for yourself and your altar space. The opening invocation used here avoids mention of Seth, as these are Osirian rites.)

Candle Rite - As you light your candle(s), say:

"Come in peace, bright Eye of Horus, come in peace.
Receive the light.
The Eye of Horus shines, like Ra in the twin Horizons, and evil hides before it. Receive the light.
The Eye of Horus destroys the enemies of Ra in all of their abodes. Receive the light.

The Eye of Horus comes, and I am purified with it.
Receive the light."

- *from the Daily Rite of Amun-Ra, Karnak, and Book of the Dead chapter 137B*

Opening Invocation – Ring your sistrum. If part of a group, everyone recites:

"Great and Little Enneads of the Gods!
Lords of Ma'at, United in Ma'at,
Great Ones who reject wrongdoing!
Assemble before the Lord of All,
And turn Your Faces toward me!
My heart is straight, my heart is open,
No darkness is in my heart!"

- *also adapted from Osiris hymn of Amunmose and hymn to Hathor in Denderah, Ancient Egyptian Literature vols. II and III*

Invocations to Osir and Anepu: *(ring sistrum)*

Iiu im hotep, Osir, neb Abju.
- Come in peace, Osiris, Lord of Abydos.

Iiu im hotep, Osir, neb Djedu.
- Come in peace, Osiris, Lord of Busiris.

Iiu im hotep, Osir, Khenti-Amentiu.
- Come in peace, Osiris, Foremost of the Westerners.

Iiu im hotep, Osir, Un-en-Nefer.
- Come in peace, Osiris, the Beatified.

Iiu im hotep, Anepu, Imi-ut.
- Come in peace, Anubis, One In His Wrappings.

Iiu im hotep, Anepu, neb Ta-Djoser.
- Come in peace, Anubis, Lord of the Sacred Land.

Iiu im hotep, Anepu, tepy dju-ef.
- Come in peace, Anubis, He on His Mountain.

Iiu im hotep, Anepu, hery seshta.
- Come in peace, Anubis, He Over the Secrets.

Offering Rite:

Water: "Take these, Your cool waters that are the Inundation."
Milk: "Milk, milk, may You taste it in Your shrine."
Incense: "I give You incense, I give You incense, great of purity."
Natron: "This is Your natron of Horus, this is Your natron of Djehuty, this is Your natron among the gods."
Food offering: "Take this, Your white loaf of the Wagy Feast.
Wine: "Receive this, Your wine on the night of Wagy."

Presentation: "Turn Yourselves to these, Your offerings; and share them with these beloved *Akhu* who are in Your care, whom I now invoke:
(read from your list of loved ones, or just name them each in turn; then ring sistrum)

"Turn yourselves to these, your offerings, which come from those who love you." *(place tray of offerings before the altar)*

Voice Offering:
Peret kheru, ta, heneket, kha khau, apdu, senotjer, merhat, khut nebet nofret wabet ankhet notjer im, en kau nib-pu, ma'a-kheru her notjer a'ah.

"A voice offering of bread, beer, a thousand of beef and poultry, incense and oil, and all good and pure things on which a god lives, for all of these *ka*s, true of voice before the Great God."
(ring sistrum)

Pouring Water for Osiris and the *Akhu*: As you pour water into your *Nun* basin for Osiris and the *akhu*, read aloud:

"This is Your cold water, Oh my father! This is Your cold water, Oh Osiris! Come to Your son, come to Horus! See, I bring it to You that You may be glad of it. See, I bring the Eye of Horus to You, that You may be glad of it. Whatever You tread under Your sandals, I will be Your guide for You. I will give You water at the Wa'g and Djehutet feasts."
- from Coffin Text 64, "Giving Water to an Akh"

You can also read from the "Hymn to Osiris" in Chapter Six, as well as Coffin Text 226, covered under the *Iru Mosyt* Rites.

(ring sistrum)

Prayer: This can be your time for silent prayer, meditation or reflection. Breathe deeply, exhale, and let the energy you've built up slowly release itself.

"Be at peace, Osir and Anepu; be at peace, beloved spirits. Peace be given for you, peace be what you see, peace be what you hear, peace be before you, peace be behind you, peace be your lot."

Closing Invocation: *(ring sistrum)*

"Great and Little Enneads of the Gods!
Great Ones before the Lord of All;
We thank You and wish You well!
Remember me, be where You like, and come again in kindness!"
- also inspired by Osiris hymn, Ancient Egyptian Literature vol. II

To conclude the rite, say: "*In-un-Ma'a*" [Truly it Is]

End of Rite

Day Three: Feast of Djehuty

(In preparation, perform the necessary purifications for yourself and your altar space.)

Candle Rite - As you light your candle(s), say:

"Come in peace, bright Eye of Horus, come in peace.
Receive the light.
The Eye of Horus shines, like Ra in the twin Horizons, and evil hides before it. Receive the light.
The Eye of Horus destroys the enemies of Ra in all of their

abodes. Receive the light.
The Eye of Horus comes, and I am purified with it.
Receive the light."

- *from the Daily Rite of Amun-Ra, Karnak, and Book of the Dead chapter 137B*

Opening Invocation – Ring your sistrum. If part of a group, everyone recites:

"Great and Little Enneads of the Gods!
Lords of Ma'at, United in Ma'at,
Great Ones who reject wrongdoing!
Assemble before the Lord of All,
And turn Your Faces toward me!
My heart is straight, my heart is open,
No darkness is in my heart!"

- *also adapted from Osiris hymn of Amunmose and hymn to Hathor in Denderah, Ancient Egyptian Literature vols. II and III*

Invocation to Djehuty: *(ring sistrum)*

Iiu im hotep, Djehuty, neb Khemnu.
- Come in peace, Djehuty, Lord of Hermopolis.

Iiu im hotep, Djehuty, neb medu netjer.
- Come in peace, Djehuty, Lord of the Sacred Words.

Iiu im hotep, Djehuty, sesh ma'a en Pesdjet.
- Come in peace, Djehuty, True Scribe of the Ennead.

Iiu im hotep, Djehuty, notjer a'ah.
- Come in peace, Djehuty, Greatest God.

Offering Rite:
Water: "Take these, Your cool waters that are the Inundation."
Milk: "Milk, milk, may You taste it in Your shrine."
Incense: "I give You incense, I give You incense, great of purity."
Natron: "This is Your natron of Horus, this is Your natron of Seth, this is Your natron among the gods."
Food offering: "Take this, Your bread on which gods live.
Sweets: "Receive this honey and sweets, Djehuty, on this

Your day of feast."
Writing tool: "Take this pen, Djehuty, True Scribe of the Ennead, on this Your day of feast."

(ring sistrum)

Presentation: "Turn Yourself to these, Your offerings, Djehuty, and receive them from me. Pass them in turn to the beloved spirits whose names You have written in the Hall of Two Truths."

Voice Offering:

Peret kheru, ta, heneket, kha khau, apdu, senotjer, merhat, khut nebet nofret wabet ankhet notjer im, en kau en... [read from your list of loved ones, or name them in turn]*...ma'a-kheru her notjer a'ah.*

"A voice offering of bread, beer, a thousand of beef and poultry, incense and oil, and all good and pure things on which a god lives, for the *ka*s of _______, true of voice before the Great God."

Blessing the Writing Tools: Place the tray with your writing tools, etc. before altar. Sweep over it slowly with a sistrum, wand, or your open hand.

"Djehuty, lord of wisdom and master of the sacred words, place Your hands upon these tools that they may do Your work, ever in beauty and truth."

(ring sistrum)

Pouring Water for Osiris and the *Akhu*: As in Day Two, for the *Wagy.*

Recitation of sacred texts - According to Plutarch, for Djehuty's festival celebrants chanted "A sweet thing is truth"; which in Egyptian would be roughly, *Iu khut nodjem ma'at.* You could also read from Chapters 94-97 of the Book of the Dead, which deal with Djehuty. Alternatively, you can recite praises for Djehuty:

Dua Djehuty, sesh ma'a en Pesdjet! - Praise Djehuty, True Scribe of the Ennead!
Dua Djehuty, iker en saret! - Praise Djehuty, Excellent of Wisdom!
Dua Djehuty, neb medu notjer! - Praise Djehuty, Lord of the Sacred Words!
Dua Djehuty, neb Khemnu! - Praise Djehuty, Lord of Khemnu!
Dua Djehuty, notjer a'ah! - Praise Djehuty, Greatest God!
Dua Djehuty, neb heka! - Praise Djehuty, Lord of Magic!
Dua Djehuty, neb Ma'at! - Praise Djehuty, Lord of Truth!
Dua Djehuty, neb pet! - Praise Djehuty, Lord of the Sky!

(ring sistrum)

Prayer: This can be your time for silent prayer, meditation or reflection. Breathe deeply, exhale, and let the energy you've built up slowly release itself.

"Praise to You, Djehuty, and thank You for Your gifts. May You continue to guide me in wisdom throughout the year."

Closing Invocation: *(ring sistrum)*

"Great and Little Enneads of the Gods!
Great Ones before the Lord of All;
We thank You and wish You well!
Remember me, be where You like, and come again in kindness!"
- also inspired by Osiris hymn, Ancient Egyptian Literature vol. II

To conclude the rite, say: "*In-un-Ma'a*" [Truly it Is]

End of Rite

The Opet Festival

Historical background: In the region of Thebes, the Opet formed a major part of the liturgical calendar, yet only the beginning and ending of the observance seem to have been public events. Theologically, the holiday observed the king's rejuvenation and re-consecration as son of Amun within the *Ipet Resyt*, or Southern Residence, temple at Karnak. The rites performed at Karnak and in Luxor were secretive and even today not well understood. Some kings actually chose to be coronated during Opet, particularly those with tenuous claims to the throne such as Horemhab, to take advantage of the legitimizing aspect of the Opet rites.

For the public, the procession of Amun's various icon statues at the beginning and end of the festival were a time of grand spectacle. A herd of sacrificial bulls was driven in the parade, their horns garlanded with flowers. Musicians sang, clapped and played sistra in the procession, dancers performed, and mass quantities of bread and beer were distributed to the crowds. At stops along the festival route, some people received oracles from various icons of Amun, as evidenced by surviving records.

The king made two public appearances during the Opet. At the first appearance water was poured on him by the gods of the four directions, represented by priests, and he proceeded into the special *per ur* ("great house") shrine to be crowned. Afterward, the rejuvenated king reappeared to the acclaim of the crowd.

Modern observance: Discussion about the role of a pharaoh in modern Kemetic practice notwithstanding, the feast of Opet can still center on renewal and rejuvenation in a spiritual sense. Its original theme of re-consecration particularly lends itself to initiations; this would be the ideal occasion for a self-dedication or initiation into a group.

You will need: Milk, food offerings and natron; ritual oil and a water vessel for anointing; if performing an initiation, supplies for the initiation rite.

Altar setup: The central figure in your Opet altar will be Amun. If you will be performing an initiation, whichever deity icons are needed for the rite should be included, either slightly below or to the side of Amun. Leave space for offerings and tools for anointing at the front of the altar or on a smaller table in front of it.

The Opet Rite

(In preparation, perform the necessary purifications for yourself and your altar space.)

Candle Rite - As you light your candle(s), say:

"Come in peace, bright Eye of Horus, come in peace. Receive the light.
The Eye of Horus shines, like Ra in the twin Horizons, and evil hides before it. Receive the light.
The Eye of Horus destroys the enemies of Ra in all of their abodes. Receive the light.
The Eye of Horus comes, and I am purified with it. Receive the light."

- *from the Daily Rite of Amun-Ra, Karnak, and Book of the Dead chapter 137B*

Opening Invocation – Ring your sistrum. If part of a group, everyone recites:

"Great Ennead of the gods who are in Iunu (yoo-NOO)!
Ra, in Your appearance at the First Time;
Ra's Twins, Shu and Tefnut;
Geb and Nut, Lord of Earth and Lady of Heaven;
Osiris [Osir], Isis [Iset], Set and Nephthys [Nebet-Hat];
Turn Your faces toward us!
Behold what is in our innermost;
Our hearts are straight, our hearts are open,
No darkness is in our hearts!"

- *adapted from Osiris hymn of Amunmose and hymn to Hathor in Denderah, Ancient Egyptian Literature vols. II and III*

Dual Invocations to Amun: *(ring sistrum)*

Iiu im hotep Amun-Ra, notjer a'ah.
- Come in peace, Amun-Ra, Greatest God.

Iiu im hotep Amun-Ra, Nisut notjeru.
- Come in peace, King of the Gods.

Iiu im hotep Amun-Ra, neb Waset.
- Come in peace, Lord of Thebes.

Iiu im hotep Amun-Ra, neb khau.
- Come in peace, Lord of Appearances.

Iiu im hotep, Amun-im-Opet, neb Ipet-Resyt.
- Come in peace, Amun in the Residence, Lord of the Southern Residence.

Iiu im hotep, Amun-im-Opet, Ka Mut-ef.
- Come in peace, Amun in the Residence, Bull of His Mother.

Iiu im hotep, Amun-im-Opet, qa'i shuty.
- Come in peace, Amun in the Residence, Tall of Plumes.

Iiu im hotep, Amun-im-Opet, notjer a'ah.
- Come in peace, Amun in the Residence, Greatest God.

Offering Rite:

Water: "Take these, Your cool waters that are the Inundation."

Milk: "Milk, milk, may You taste it in Your shrine."

Incense: "I give You incense, I give You incense, great of purity."

Natron: "This is Your natron of Horus, this is Your natron of Djehuty, this is Your natron among the gods."

Food: "Take this, Your bread, on which gods live."

Wine: "Receive this, oh Amun, Your wine on the Feast of Opet."

Presentation: Turn Yourself to these, Your offerings, oh Amun, on this Your feast of Opet.

(ring sistrum)

Ritual Action: If you will be performing a self-dedication or initiation, do so now. If you are using the one provided in Chapter 4, skip the offering portion, as it has just been covered in the Opet Rites.

Rite of Rejuvenation: Using your pinkie finger, anoint the forehead of the icon of Amun with oil. For the water, you can either use your finger again, very carefully pour a small amount onto the statue, or simply hold up a saucer of water.

Oil: "Hail, Amun, and take this oil, which is the Eye of Horus. Let its scent reach You, let it rejuvenate You, let it cool Your heart. You shall not grow weary with it."

Water: "Hail, Amun, and receive these cool waters, which are the Eye of Horus. May they rejuvenate You, may they purify You, may they cool Your heart, for You shall not grow weary with them."

Reversion: Now anoint yourself, and other participants if present, on the forehead with oil.

"Oil, oil, where should you be? You were on the forehead of Horus, but now I will place you upon this forehead of mine." (or, "the foreheads of these.")

"Receive these cool waters, so that you may be purified and refreshed."
- adapted from Pyramid Text 77 and the Daily Rite of Amun-Ra, Karnak

Divination: Many records survive of citizens seeking oracles from Amun during the Opet festivities. If you wish to perform a divination centered on Amun, do so now.

Opet Hymn to Amun: *(ring sistrum)*

Hail, Oh Amun-Ra,
Lord of Thrones of the Two Lands,
May You live forever!
A drinking place is hewn out,
The sky folded back to the south.

A drinking place is hewn out,
The sky folded back to the north.

Hail, Oh Amun-Ra,
First One of the Two Lands,
Foremost One in Karnak,
In splendid appearance in Your fleet,
In Your beautiful Feast of Opet,
May You be pleased with it!
A drinking place is built
For You in the ship of ships.
The paths of the Twin Horizons
Have been bound up for You;
A great flood has been raised up.
May You pacify the Two Ladies,
Oh Lord of the Red and White crowns,
Oh Horus strong of arm!

- *from the Opet reliefs at Karnak, in The Life of Meresamun*

(ring sistrum)

Prayer: This can be your time for silent prayer, meditation or reflection. Breathe deeply, exhale, and let the energy you've built up slowly release itself.

Closing Invocation: *(ring sistrum)*
"Great Ennead of the gods in Iunu!
Ra, in Your appearance at the First Time;
Ra's Twins, Shu and Tefnut;
Geb and Nut, Lord of Earth and Lady of Heaven;
Osiris [Osir], Isis [Iset], Set and Nephthys [Nebet-Hat];
I thank You, and wish You well!
Remember me, be where You like, and come again in kindness!
Seneb-ti!"

- *inspired from Osiris hymn of Amunmose*

To conclude the rite, say: "*In-un-Ma'a*" [Truly it Is]

End of Rite

Sailing of Hathor - *Khenut Hat-Hor*

Historical background: This feast was also called the Feast of Hathor, "Mistress of the North Wind". Possibly playing on the recurring theme of the Return of the Distant Goddess, the festival honored Hathor with water and land processions. Families played tambourines and clappers and offered flowers and food to Hathor. Prayers in graffiti at Hathor's chapel in Deir el-Bahari refer to a "Day of Doing Good" (*Heru Pa'Ir Nofer*), which may have been associated with the Sailing of Hathor; although references elsewhere address Ptah or Sakhmet, so the "Day of Doing Good" may not have been unique to Hathor. Another possible reference to this feast mentions Hathor's "Feast of Entering the Sky" (*Hab Aq nu Pet*).

Occurring during the month of Hathor, or Akhet III, the feast was a major month-long event at Denderah. Passages in texts also refer to Hathor of the "Red Linen" or the "Red Dress", and the "Festival of the Red Linen" may have been associated with Hathor's festivities. Another of the smaller observances at Denderah during that month was the "Feast of Opening the Bosoms of Women", and actually involved a procession with a phallus figure!

Modern observance: Hathor's feast of sailing can draw upon the themes of doing good deeds and returning what was lost, as well as merriment or (where appropriate) fertility. The female element will obviously be strong in this feast; if you plan a group observance, let female members lead a procession around the altar or play instruments. Put a little "girl power" into your celebration.

You will need: Milk, food offerings, natron, ritual oil, sistrum, flowers, and beer, if available.

Altar setup: Hathor will figure as the central element of the altar. Look in craft or curio stores for a wooden canoe or boat; painted in green or gold with a pair of *udjat* eyes on the prow, it can provide a model bark for the "Sailing" of Hathor. Blue altar cloth can suggest the sky or celestial waters. You will also need red cloth to offer Hathor; if you're artistically inclined, make Her icon a red shawl. Be sure to incorporate flowers into the altar decorations.

The Khenut Hat-Hor Rite

(In preparation, perform the necessary purifications for yourself and your altar space. If observing as a group, start with sistrum-playing or singing, such as the Hymn to Hathor in Chapter 6.)

Candle Rite - As you light your candle(s), say:

"Come in peace, bright Eye of Horus, come in peace.
Receive the light.
The Eye of Horus shines, like Ra in the twin Horizons, and evil hides before it. Receive the light.
The Eye of Horus destroys the enemies of Ra in all of their abodes. Receive the light.
The Eye of Horus comes, and I am purified with it.
Receive the light."

- *from the Daily Rite of Amun-Ra, Karnak, and Book of the Dead chapter 137B*

Opening Invocation – Ring your sistrum. If part of a group, everyone recites:
"Great Ennead of the gods who are in Iunu (yoo-NOO)!
Ra, in Your appearance at the First Time;
Ra's Twins, Shu and Tefnut;
Geb and Nut, Lord of Earth and Lady of Heaven;
Osiris [Osir], Isis [Iset], Set and Nephthys (NEF-tis) [Nebet-Hat];
Turn Your faces toward us!
Behold what is in our innermost;
Our hearts are straight, our hearts are open,
No darkness is in our hearts!"

- *adapted from Osiris hymn of Amunmose and hymn to Hathor in Denderah, Ancient Egyptian Literature vols. II and III*

Invocation to Hat-Hor: *(ring sistrum)*

Iiu im hotep, Hat-Hor, nebet Mehyt.
- Come in peace, Hathor, Mistress of the North Wind.

Iiu im hotep, Hat-Hor, Irit en Ra.
- Come in peace, Hathor, Eye of Ra.

Iiu im hotep, Hat-Hor, nebet nub.
- Come in peace, Hathor, Lady of Gold.

Iiu im hotep, Hat-Hor, nebet pet.
- Come in peace, Hathor, Mistress of the Sky.

Offering Rite:
Water: "Take these, Your cool waters that are the Inundation."
Milk: "Milk, milk, may You taste it in Your shrine."
Incense: "I give You incense, I give You incense, great of purity."
Natron: "This is Your natron of Horus, this is Your natron of Djehuty, this is Your natron among the gods."
Ointment: "Receive this ointment, from the forehead of Ra."
Food: "Take this, Your bread, on which gods live."
Flowers: "Take these flowers, that they may refresh You."
Beer: "Receive this beer that is pleasing to Your heart on this, Your day of sailing."

Offering the Sistrum: *(ring sistrum)*
Your sistrum for You,
Oh Mighty One,
Great Flame, Oh Shining One,
The sistrum to quench Your ire.
- adapted from Edfu relief texts

Presentation: Turn Yourself to these, Your offerings, Lady Hat-Hor, and receive them from me; may Your heart take joy in them.

(ring sistrum)

Offering the Red Dress for Hathor - Present the red cloth or shawl to Hathor and read aloud:

"The mountain is broken, the stone is split, the Eastern Horizon is opened for Hathor!
I am the one who follows Ihy, I have come to the place where my mistress is so that I may see Her beauty and give Her the dress.
The Dress of Hathor Is Woven.
I kiss the earth, I worship my mistress, I have seen Her beauty. I give praise to Hathor, for I have seen Her beauty. I give Her the dress, Her shape is distinguished above the Gods, and I see Her beauty."
- adapted from Coffin Texts 483 and 484, 486

If observing as a group, let female members lead a circumambulation around the altar or procession; ring sistrums and chant hymn throughout.

Hymn of the Sistrum:
I take the sistrum,
I take the sistrum,
I dispel evil.
I drive off anger
From the Eye of Ra,
Like Ihy who plays
For the Golden One
To Her heart's content!
- adapted from Denderah relief texts

(ring sistrum)

Prayer - Iru Nofer (Doing Good): Use this time to offer prayers or requests for intercession to Hathor. You can write them down on a clean piece of paper and put them in a blue bowl in front of Her icon. Let this be your time for silent prayer, meditation or reflection. Breathe deeply, exhale, and let the energy you've built up slowly release itself.

(ring sistrum)

"Come in peace, Oh Beautiful One; come in peace, Lady of Gold. May You remain close by me, as You remain close by the side of Your father, Ra. Be at peace, Lady Hathor!"

Closing Invocation: *(ring sistrum)*

"Great Ennead of the gods in Iunu!
Ra, in Your appearance at the First Time;
Ra's Twins, Shu and Tefnut;
Geb and Nut, Lord of Earth and Lady of Heaven;
Osiris [Osir], Isis [Iset], Set and Nephthys [Nebet-Hat];
I thank You, and wish You well!
Remember me, be where You like, and come again in kindness!
Seneb-ti!"

- *inspired from Osiris hymn of Amunmose*

To conclude the rite, say: "*In-un-Ma'a*" [Truly it Is]

End of Rite

The Feast of Sokar

Historical background: The Feast of Sokar had a long evolution. A primitive form of it was known from the Archaic Period. It took its classic form during the Old Kingdom, but into the New Kingdom it began to meld with the Feast of Osiris. By Ptolemaic times the two festivals had merged completely. As Sokar, a chthonic god, came to be associated with Ptah and Osiris, the two similarly-themed planting festivals devoted to Sokar and to Osiris also syncretized.

Commemorating the burial and resurrection of Sokar, the observance included a "Night of *Notjeryt*" (*Gereh Notjeryt*) in which people kept an overnight vigil, possibly at the tombs of their loved ones. It was also known as the "Day of Tying Onions", and people tied garlands of onions roughly resembling *lei*'s to wear around their necks and offer to the deceased. A statue of the Deir el-Medina artisan Kha, found in his intact tomb, still has such a garland around its shoulders. Onions, whose bulbs grow underground, symbolized food for the deceased.

Another part of the funerary rites was "Hacking Up the Earth" (*hebes ta*). Inscriptions depict the king performing a similar act, perhaps as a ceremonial groundbreaking before planting began. But references from the Pyramid Texts through the Book of the Dead also refer to earth being 'hacked up' for the spirits of the dead. This may have been meant to invoke Sokar's, and later Osiris', dominion over the ground and the Underworld.

Elite men of the king's court vied for the privilege of participating in processions that took place around the walls of the city, either Memphis in the north or the *Akhmenu* at Karnak in the south. The king, statues of Hathor, Wadjit, Shesmetet (a goddess associated with wine pressing), Bastet and Sakhmet as well as heraldric standards all took part, but the highlight of the procession was Sokar in his *Henu*-bark. An elaborately stylized boat ornamented with an antelope's head and mounted on a sledge, it carried Sokar's icon statue in the shape of a mummiform falcon. Known as "Going Around the Walls", the procession heralded Sokar's triumphal resurrection. Musicians, singers and priests - including the courtiers who successfully wrangled a position in the festival - censed and poured libations before Sokar's *Henu* bark. Participants in the procession shouted, "Victory, victory, oh Sovereign!"

Modern observance: The Feast of Sokar, like the Osiris Mysteries, focuses on honoring the dead. Sokar's observance has an added benefit for devotees of Seth (a.k.a. Sutekh), since it does not involve veiled references to Osiris' murder. Followers of Seth can observe Sokar's feast night without contradicting the veneration of their patron.

You will need: Milk, water, wine, food offerings, natron; green onions and raffia tape or string; seven vessels or vases to serve as the Seven Vessels of Ka-Hor-Ka, each containing water or other liquid offerings, and a larger bowl to receive the liquids; a small pot of earth and spade, plus a few grain seeds to plant in the earth; and a red ceramic bowl, pot or plate.

Altar setup: Images of Sokar are hard to find. One local group addressed the problem by using a figure of a "mummy falcon"; another option is to use a statue of the composite Ptah-Sokar-Osiris, which can be found online.

Because of the potentially copious amounts of offerings, in the form of food, vessels, and tied onions, consider setting up a smaller table in front of the main altar. Make sure you have space for "hacking up the earth" and "smashing of the red pot" in front of your altar space. Place the red pot on the ground inside your ritual space, off of the altar itself.

Gereh Notjeryt - Tying the Onions

The night before you observe the Feast of Sokar, tie your onion garlands. Light a candle and offer incense before beginning. You can also chant as you work, "White teeth of Horus, Sound Eye of Horus"; onion bulbs were regarded as the teeth of Horus as well as a life-giving offering to the deceased.

The Feast of Sokar Rite

(In preparation, perform the necessary purifications for yourself and your altar space. The Osirian invocation is used here, but you have the option to adapt.)

Candle Rite - As you light your candle(s), say:

"Come in peace, bright Eye of Horus, come in peace.
Receive the light.
The Eye of Horus shines, like Ra in the twin Horizons, and evil hides before it. Receive the light.
The Eye of Horus destroys the enemies of Ra in all of their abodes. Receive the light.
The Eye of Horus comes, and I am purified with it.
Receive the light."

- from the Daily Rite of Amun-Ra, Karnak, and Book of the Dead chapter 137B

Opening Invocation – Ring your sistrum. If part of a group, everyone recites:

"Great and Little Enneads of the Gods!
Lords of Ma'at, United in Ma'at,
Great Ones who reject wrongdoing!
Assemble before the Lord of All,
And turn Your Faces toward me!
My heart is straight, my heart is open,
No darkness is in my heart!"

- *also from Ancient Egyptian Literature vols. II and III*

Invocation to Sokar: *(ring sistrum)*

Iiu im hotep, Sokar, neb Rosetau.
- Come in peace, Sokar, Lord of Rosetau.

Iiu im hotep, Sokar, neb neheh.
- Come in peace, Sokar, Lord of Eternity.

Iiu im hotep, Sokar, heqa Iugaret.
- Come in peace, Sokar, Ruler of the Land of Silence.

Iiu im hotep, Sokar, neb kereret.
- Come in peace, Sokar, Lord of the Cavern.

Offering Rite:

Water: "Take these, Your cool waters that are the Inundation."
Milk: "Milk, milk, may You taste it in Your shrine."
Incense: "I give You incense, I give You incense, great of purity."
Natron: "This is Your natron of Horus, this is Your natron of Djehuty, this is Your natron among the gods."
Food: "Take this, Your bread, on which gods live."
Wine: "Receive this, Your wine on Your night of feast."

(ring sistrum)

Reversion: "Turn Yourself to these, Your offerings, oh Sokar, Lord of Rosetau; and share them with our Blessed Dead who are in Your Land of Silence:"
Name the *akhu* you will be honoring and place your onion garland on the offering table. If observing as a group, have each participant place their onion garland on the offering table and speak the name(s) of their loved ones; ring sistrums after each person speaks.

(ring sistrum)

Voice Offering:

Peret kheru, ta, heneket, kha khau, apdu, senotjer, merhat, khut nebet nofret wabet ankhet notjer im, en kau en... [read from your list of loved ones, or name them in turn]*...ma'a-kheru her notjer a'ah.*

"A voice offering of bread, beer, a thousand of beef and poultry, incense and oil, and all good and pure things on which a god lives, for the *ka*s of _______, true of voice before the Great God."

(ring sistrum)

The Seven Vessels of Ha-Hor-Ka:
Pour from each of the seven vessels into the bowl on the offering table. If observing as a group, have participants pour from the vessels. As you or the participants pour, say aloud:

"Hail, oh Sokar, and receive these Seven Vessels of Ka-Hor-Ka, that You may taste of them and they may cool Your heart. May the hearts of our Blessed Dead be cooled with them in turn."

Hoe-ing the Earth:
Ceremonially hoe the earth in the pot, placing grain seeds into the dirt and then pouring the contents of the bowl over them.

Smashing the Red Pot - Take the red vessel and say:

"This is the Sound Eye of Horus; it has been set for You, that You may be strong, and evil be afraid of you." *- from Pyramid Text 244*
(smash pot)

Paher-ef Inbu (Going Around the Walls): This by necessity is a group activity. Select a volunteer to take the icon of Sokar and lead a circumambulation around the altar space. Drumming and sistrum playing is highly encouraged! The procession will circle four times. The group can chant, "Victory, victory oh sovereign!", or use a call-and-answer from this hymn:

"Hail, Sokar, lord of Rosetau!
Hail, oh golden remedy!
Hail, Sokar, keeper of caverns!
Hail, Lord of Eternity!

Sokar, take hold of Your shrine!
Sokar, take hold of Your temple!
Sokar, take hold of Your offerings!
Sokar, take hold of Your city!

Sokar is crowned, Lord of the Feast!
Sokar is crowned, Lord of the Feast!"
- adapted from the Hymn to Osiris-Sokar, The Burden of Isis

(ring sistrum when procession stops)

Prayer: This can be your time for silent prayer, meditation or reflection. Breathe deeply, exhale, and let the energy you've built up slowly release itself.

Closing Invocation: *(ring sistrum)*

"Great and Little Enneads of the Gods!
Great Ones before the Lord of All;
We thank You and wish You well!
Remember me, be where You like, and come again in kindness!"
- also inspired by Osiris hymn, Ancient Egyptian Literature vol. II

To conclude the rite, say: "*In-un-Ma'a*" [Truly it Is]

End of Rite

Khoiakh Mysteries

Historical background: *Khoiakh* is the Greek equivalent of *Ka-Her-Ka*, or "*Ka* upon *Ka*", the festival which lent its name to the last month of Akhet. Generally this refers to the Osiris Mysteries, although records from Deir el-Medina also mention bringing a ritual set of "Seven Vessels of *Ka-Her-Ka*" to a shrine of the goddess Meretseger located in the Valley of the Kings.

A major component of the Osiris Mysteries was the *Haker* Feast. In Abydos this included a procession led by the standard of Wepwawet and by *sem* priests, who were involved in the repulsion of Osiris' enemies. The procession led along an ancient *wadi* (like a gully or an arroyo) into Poker, where the tomb of Osiris was said to be located. So sacred was the processional route that an inscription dating to the Thirteenth Dynasty threatened anyone who built a structure blocking the processional path with burning: the order was heeded until Ptolemaic times.

On the night of *Haker*, a vigil was held in which Horus was said to commune with his father Osiris. Secret rites were performed overnight, and the following morning Osiris made a triumphal return to the temple. In Thebes, a similar procession was made that included two "corn mummies" and a heraldric standard of Osiris, consisting of a wig topped with two plumes mounted on a pole.

Through the Late Period and into Greco-Roman times, the Osiris Mysteries overtook the older Feast of Sokar and became increasingly elaborate. Multiple Osiris chapels were set up in the precincts of Karnak; at Denderah, Osiris chapels were commissioned by Cleopatra VII. During the portion of the festival commemorating Osiris' burial, secret rituals were performed that involved making "mummies" of Osiris and Sokar according to specific recipes of earth, stones, myrrh and semiprecious stones. The mummy mixtures, before being pressed into molds, dried and "embalmed", were presented to either a statue or actress representing Nut, mother of Osiris. Special liturgies were chanted for each stage of the process, such as "Protection of the Bed" and execration rites against Apophis.

The funerary processions for the Osiris and Sokar mummies in Thebes made their way through most of the major shrines of Karnak and included several interludes of nocturnal water processions on the temple lakes before stopping at a shrine considered to be the Tomb of Osiris. One papyrus record, Papyrus N 3176, actually gives instructions for the procession such as when to walk fast or slow. At one point it calls for an astronomer-priest to shout, "There is no god!" The crowd accompanying cries out in return, "Don't take him away from us!" Liturgical songs recorded in the Bremner-Rhind Papyrus were meant to accompany the rituals and the procession. The Songs of Isis and Nephthys included parts sung in unison, parts sung antiphonically (call-and-answer), and parts interspersed with pronouncements by the priests. The festival-goers following the procession accompanied their songs with hand drums and probably clapping.

At the Tomb of Osiris (in various temples), the previous year's Osiris and Sokar effigies were carefully removed and ceremoniously buried in a special vault. The newly "embalmed" models were put in their place, to represent Osiris-Sokar for the next year. Other icons of Osiris may have been taken in a final water procession; another part of the festival called for miniature boats with images of Osiris to be floated, along with 365 oil lamps, on the sacred lake.

Modern observance: Khoiakh, being the quintessential Egyptian festival of the dead, shares commonalities with Samhain and Dia de los Muertes. If you draw upon Samhain, Halloween or Dia de los Muertes elements for your observance, try to avoid skull-and-bone or "mummy" motifs. The Egyptians avoided graphic representations or descriptions of Osiris' death for fear of perpetuating it. They focused instead on his regeneration and resurrection. However, jack-o-lanterns and harvest decor can integrate quite elegantly into an altar. If you have pictures or tokens of departed loved ones, include those as well. This feast is for them, too.

You will need: Milk, water, bread, ritual oil, natron; black and white cups, ritual adze; red ceramic pot; a *Djed* emblem. If at a loss for a *Djed* representation, try using a corn sheaf, which can often be found at grocery or craft stores in the fall. One theory about the origin of the *Djed* pillar interprets it as a stylized sheaf of grain.

Altar setup: An Osiris icon will be the central focus of the altar, with space for offerings and Opening of the Mouth implements in front and slightly below. If you make an *Imiut*, place it to the side of the altar. Put the red pottery vessel on the ground inside your ritual space, off of the altar itself. Leave space for the smashing of the pot, and warn any observers to keep back for that part of the ritual; in our circle, one year someone found ceramic shards in her hair after the ritual!

Note the Imiut *emblem, and jack o'lantern, in this altar for the Osiris Mysteries. Author's photo.*

The *Khoiakh* Rite

(In preparation, perform the necessary purifications for yourself and your altar space. The Osirian invocation is used here.)

Candle Rite - As you light your candle(s), say:

"Come in peace, bright Eye of Horus, come in peace.
Receive the light.
The Eye of Horus shines, like Ra in the twin Horizons, and evil hides before it. Receive the light.
The Eye of Horus destroys the enemies of Ra in all of their abodes. Receive the light.
The Eye of Horus comes, and I am purified with it.
Receive the light."

- *from the Daily Rite of Amun-Ra, Karnak, and Book of the Dead chapter 137B*

Opening Invocation – Ring your sistrum. If part of a group, everyone recites:
"Great and Little Enneads of the Gods!
Lords of Ma'at, United in Ma'at,
Great Ones who reject wrongdoing!
Assemble before the Lord of All,
And turn Your Faces toward me!
My heart is straight, my heart is open,
No darkness is in my heart!"

- *also from Ancient Egyptian Literature vols. II and III*

Invocation to Osir: *(ring sistrum)*
Iiu im hotep, Osir, neb Abju.
- Come in peace, Osiris, Lord of Abydos.

Iiu im hotep, Osir, neb Djedu.
- Come in peace, Osiris, Lord of Busiris.

Iiu im hotep, Osir, Khenti-Amentiu.
- Come in peace, Osiris, Foremost of the Westerners.

Iiu im hotep, Osir, Un-en-Nefer.
- Come in peace, Osiris, the Beatified.

Opening of the Mouth Rite:

Libation: These your cool waters, Osiris, have come from your son Horus.
I have come bringing Horus' eye, that your heart may be cooled with it; I have placed it at your feet. Your heart will not grow weary of it.

(*offer water*) Come, you have been invoked. *(four times)*

Incense: I give you incense, I give you incense, great of purity. Let its scent reach you and purify you. (*Each offers incense on burner*)

Cleansing the Mouth: This is your natron of Horus, this is your natron of Djehuty. This is your own natron among the gods. You are purified with it. (O*ffer natron*) Your mouth is clean as a calf's on the day it is born.

Milk, milk that parts your mouth, may you taste it in your shrine. That of Horus, that of Djehuty, that of the two gods reconciled, milk. (*pour milk*)

Opening the mouth and eyes: (*touch statue's face with striker*) I have fixed your jaws spread for you; let me part your mouth for you.

Osiris, take this, Horus' eye which had departed; I have returned it so that you may take it to your mouth. This is the breast of Horus' body *(raise jug of milk);* this is the breast of Isis, that she may suckle you. *(pour milk)*

(raise cups) Here are Horus' two eyes, black and white; lift them to your face, and illuminate it. *(set cups on altar)*

Anointing: Ointment, ointment, from the forehead of Ra; I shall put it on you and it shall transfigure you. (*anoint statue with oil*)

Offering and reversion: At peace for you shall be Ra in the dawn. Peace be given for you, peace be what you see, peace be what you hear, peace be before you, peace be behind you, peace be your lot. (o*ffer bread*)

Turn Yourself to these, Your offerings, oh Osir; and share them with these beloved *Akhu* who are with You in Duat.

Voice offering:

Peret kheru, ta, heneket, kha khau, apdu, senotjer, merhat, khut nebet nofret wabet ankhet notjer im, en kau en... [read from your list of loved ones, or name them in turn]*...ma'a-kheru her notjer a'ah.*

"A voice offering of bread, beer, a thousand of beef and poultry, incense and oil, and all good and pure things on which a god lives, for the *ka*s of _______, true of voice before the Great God."

(ring sistrum)

Raising of the *Djed*: Raise an image of the Djed on the altar in front of Osiris. Read aloud the Hymn for Raising the *Djed*:

"To Your *ka*, the sistrum, and to Your kindly face, the *menit* and *sekhem* as You arise, Oh august *Djed*, Osiris-Sokar, Lord of Shetyt!

Osiris-Sokar appears in glory;
Praised are You now!
Exalted are You, Oh Rudder.
You join with the land
That You may travel through it.
May Ra favor You for Your goodness.
Come, let us exalt him!

You have filled the Two Lands with Your beauty,
Radiant and reborn as the sun in the sky!"

– *adapted from the Ramesseum Dramatic Papyrus and the tomb of Kheru-ef*

Smashing of the Pot: "This is the Sound Eye of Horus; it has been set for you that you may grow strong." *- from Pyramid Text 244*
(smash pot)

(ring sistrum)

Prayer: This is your time for silent prayer, meditation or reflection. Breathe deeply, exhale, and let the energy you've built up slowly release itself.

"Be at peace, Osir; be at peace, beloved spirits. Remember me, as I have remembered you; protect me, as I have protected you."

Closing Invocation: *(ring sistrum)*

"Great and Little Enneads of the Gods!
Great Ones before the Lord of All;
We thank You and wish You well!
Remember me, be where You like, and come again in kindness!"

- also inspired by Osiris hymn, Ancient Egyptian Literature vol. II

To conclude the rite, say: "*In-un-Ma'a*" [Truly it Is]

End of Rite

Imiut *detail. Author's photo.*

Feasts of Neheb-Kau, Coronation of the Sacred Falcon

Following the Khoiakh observances and marking the start of *Peret*, the planting season, was the Rebirth Feast of Neheb-kau. Neheb-kau was a deity of time and of fate, pictured as one of two serpents at either side of the throne of Sakhmet or Bast. Perhaps because of this association, the major focus of celebration for the Neheb-Kau feast was actually Sakhmet. Records at Deir el-Medina also refer to Meret-seger, their local patroness, receiving rites for the occasion of Neheb-kau. Given these associations, the theme of the festival seems to have been redemption and rebirth, particularly for the dead; some New Kingdom texts refer to the names of deceased who are "not to be forgotten on the morning of Neheb-Kau".

In the region of Edfu, the start of Peret I was observed with the Coronation of the Sacred Falcon. A live falcon was carried in a silent procession led by priests wearing masks to represent the Four Sons of Horus in their aspects as the Souls of Nekhen and Pe. The procession went to a special temple enclosure where the live falcon was crowned before the icon statue of Horus. The reigning king offered meat to Horus, which may have been eaten by the live falcon. Recorded on the walls of the Edfu temple is the Book of Appeasing Sakhmet, which invoked her protection of Horus and the ruling king against the Seven Arrows of the Year. This was chanted during the Coronation of the Sacred Falcon, harking back to the ceremonies done at the start of the year.

Sed Festival - *Hab Sed*

Historical background: If a pharaoh lived long enough, at his thirtieth year on the throne he would celebrate a special jubilee known as the *Hab Sed*. Some kings observed a *Hab Sed* earlier in their reign, for various reasons; others ruled long enough to have one, but their jubilees were only summarily observed. As one of the oldest festivals in Egyptian history, the *Hab Sed* was a highly tradition-oriented occasion.

Sed may refer to an ancient jackal deity represented on standards which were carried in the *Hab Sed* processions; this 'Sed' may be another identity of Wepwawet. These standards were carried by the "Servants of the Souls of Nekhen and Pe" (*hem bau Nekhen*

Pe), and they preceded the king as he ran or walked a course between sets of crescent-shaped markers. This probably acted as a symbolic circumambulation of the king's domain. Other iconic elements of the *Sed* festival included a tall staircase leading to double thrones in a booth, which symbolized the king's rule over the double kingdoms of Upper and Lower Egypt. Amunhotep III added Osirian elements to his *Hab Sed*, including raising a *Djed* pillar and driving cattle and asses around it, as well as hosting mock battles against the enemies of Sokar-Osiris. Gifts were given to his officials, who wore green fillets around their heads, perhaps evoking rejuvenation.

Modern observances: Again, the debate of over modern pharaohs aside, Hab Sed might not serve as a relevant observance unless you choose to commemorate a historical pharaoh, such as Tutankhamun or Rameses the Great. Feasting to Sakhmet and honoring loved ones could also mark the occasion. Honoring the Coronation of the Sacred Falcon would have to be modified owing to the difficulty - and legality! - of obtaining a live falcon. One alternative might be to sponsor a peregrine falcon, now listed as an endangered species, at a zoo or wildlife rescue. For the example given here, Horus and Sakhmet are honored together.

You will need: Milk; food offerings, including meat; wine and natron; a model *peschent*, or red and white Dual Crown, for Horus, and optional green ribbons to wear as headbands for the observance.

Altar setup: Put icons of Sakhmet and Horus at the center of your altar, leaving room for offerings in front. Look for Super Sculpy or modeling clay to make the model crown for Horus; it doesn't have to fit his head (unless the icon happens not to have anything on its head already), but leave room to place it at his feet. When making Horus' model crown, don't forget the curl on it; that represents the goddesses Wadjit and Sakhmet, and can easily be made with wire or a decorative twist tie.

A Coronation of the Sacred Falcon Rite

(In preparation, perform the necessary purifications for yourself and your altar space.)

Candle Rite - As you light your candle(s), say:

"Come in peace, bright Eye of Horus, come in peace.
Receive the light.
The Eye of Horus shines, like Ra in the twin Horizons, and evil hides before it. Receive the light.
The Eye of Horus destroys the enemies of Ra in all of their abodes. Receive the light.
The Eye of Horus comes, and I am purified with it. Receive the light."

- *from the Daily Rite of Amun-Ra, Karnak, and Book of the Dead chapter 137B*

Opening Invocation – Ring your sistrum. If part of a group, everyone recites:

"Great Ennead of the gods who are in Iunu (yoo-NOO)!
Ra, in Your appearance at the First Time;
Ra's Twins, Shu and Tefnut;
Geb and Nut, Lord of Earth and Lady of Heaven;
Osiris [Osir], Isis [Iset], Set and Nephthys (NEF-tis) [Nebet-Hat];
Turn Your faces toward us!
Behold what is in our innermost;
Our hearts are straight, our hearts are open,
No darkness is in our hearts!"

- *adapted from Osiris hymn of Amunmose and hymn to Hathor in Denderah, Ancient Egyptian Literature vols. II and III*

Invocations to Horus and Sakhmet: *(ring sistrum)*

Iiu im hotep, Horu, neb Behdet.
- Come in peace, Horus, Lord of Behdet.

Iiu im hotep, Horu, Ba Iabty.
- Come in peace, Horus, Soul of the East.

Iiu im hotep, Horu, sab shuty.
- Come in peace, Horus, One of Dappled Plumage.

Iiu im hotep, Horu, notjer a'ah.
- Come in peace, Horus, Greatest God.

Iiu im hotep, Sakhmet, nebet senedjet.
- Come in peace, Sakhmet, Mistress of Fear.

Iiu im hotep, Sakhmet, Khenti Per-Neser.
- Come in peace, Sakhmet, Foremost of the House of Flame.

Iiu im hotep, Sakhmet, nebet Tawy.
- Come in peace, Sakhmet, Mistress of the Two Lands.

Iiu im hotep, Sakhmet, notjerit a'ah.
- Come in peace, Sakhmet, Greatest Goddess.

Offering Rite:
Water: "Take these, Your cool waters that are the Inundation."
Milk: "Milk, milk, may You taste it in Your shrine."
Incense: "I give You incense, I give You incense, great of purity."
Natron: "This is Your natron of Horus, this is Your natron of Djehuty, this is Your natron among the gods'."
Food offering: "Take this, Your bread on which gods live."
Meat offering: "Accept this meat, oh Horus, that none may oppose You."
Wine: "Receive this, Your wine on this happy day of Your coronation."

Presentation: "Turn Yourself to these, Your offerings, oh Horus and Sakhmet, on this Your day of feast."

Offerings to the *Akhu*: At this point, you can include a Voice Offering to the blessed dead, and a water offering; see the rite for Feast of the Valley further below.

Invocation to Sakhmet - This is a variation of the *Sehotep Sakhmet* Litany from the Epagomenal Days and New Year's, concentrating on Horus:

1) Hail, Sakhmet, Who presides over the land, Lady of Flourishing, Generous One, Sakhmet who protects the Two Lands! Come to Your son Horus who is under Your sway! Save Him, protect Him, and preserve Him from the First Arrow of the Year!

2) Hail, Sakhmet, oh Curl, oh Hidden Lady, Wadjit the Great! Come to Your son Horus who is under Your sway! Save Him, protect Him, and preserve Him from the First Arrow of the Year!

3) Hail, Sakhmet, who moves in light, who terrifies the gods with Her massacre! Come to Your son Horus who is under Your sway! Save Him, protect Him, and preserve Him from the First Arrow of the Year!

4) Hail, Sakhmet, who guides mankind, Lady of the Dual Shores, Mistress of humanity! Come to Your son Horus who is under Your sway! Save Him, protect Him, and preserve Him from the First Arrow of the Year!

5) Hail, Sakhmet, Great Shining One, Foremost in the Mansion of Flame *(Per Neser)*, Who terrorizes the Two Lands with fear! Come to Your son Horus who is under Your sway! Save Him, protect Him, and preserve Him from the First Arrow of the Year!

6) Hail, Sakhmet, who loves Ma'at and hates *isfet*, Lady of the people! Come to Your son Horus who is under Your sway! Save Him, protect Him, and preserve Him from the First Arrow of the Year!

7) Hail, Sakhmet, Uraeus who opens the acacia, Great and Sovereign One! Come to Your son Horus who is under Your sway! Save Him, protect Him, and preserve Him from the First Arrow of the Year!

- *adapted from Richard Reidy's translation from the French from* Sekhmet et la Protection du Monde *by Phillippe Germond*

(ring sistrum)

Presentation of the Crown: In ancient times, the processional part of the Coronation rite was performed in total silence. Here, offer the crown to Horus in silent reverence. When you are done, ring your sistrum or sound any other instrument you might have.

Four Annunciations of Horus:

Hail, Duamutef, Lord of the East!
Horus is crowned, Lord of Nekhen! *(ring sistrum)*

Hail, Qebehsenuef, Lord of the West!
Horus is crowned, Lord of Upper Egypt! *(ring sistrum)*

Hail, Hapy, Lord of the North!
Horus is crowned, Lord of Pe (PAY)! *(ring sistrum)*

Hail, Imsety, Lord of the South!
Horus is crowned, Lord of Lower Egypt! *(ring sistrum)*

Prayer: This can be your time for silent prayer, meditation or reflection. Breathe deeply, exhale, and let the energy you've built up slowly release itself.

Closing Invocation: *(ring sistrum)*

"Great Ennead of the gods in Iunu!
Ra, in Your appearance at the First Time;
Ra's Twins, Shu and Tefnut;
Geb and Nut, Lord of Earth and Lady of Heaven;
Osiris [Osir], Isis [Iset], Set and Nephthys [Nebet-Hat];
I thank You, and wish You well!
Remember me, be where You like, and come again in kindness!
Seneb-ti!"

- *inspired from Osiris hymn of Amunmose*

To conclude the rite, say: "*In-un-Ma'a*" [Truly it Is]

End of Rite

Sailing of Mut - *Khenut Mut*

Historical background: Celebrated at the end of Peret I, the Sailing of Mut was also called *Ta' Abet*, or "Great Offering", from which the month name *Ta'ib* derives. A predominantly Theban festival, it was similar to the Sailing of Hathor. Food and unguent jars were presented to Mut, ritual libations were poured and much singing and drinking was done. Mut appeared in her sacred bark on the *Isheru*, or sacred lake, at her temple in Karnak; the popular woman's name *Mutemwia*, "Mut in [Her] Bark", referred to her festival appearance.

Mut's water procession probably took place during the day, but hymns to Hathor referring to the latter goddess' feast refer to drinking and celebrating through the night by torchlight along the shore. The feast of Mut may have transpired in similar fashion. Like the Sailing of Hathor, Mut's festival alludes to her role in the Theban tradition as the Eye of Ra who returns placated from her desert rampage.

Modern observance: Its close similarity to the Sailing of Hathor could potentially become repetitious. Depending on which goddesses you honor, you could simply pick the one you prefer to celebrate; remember, not all ancient localities observed the same feasts. The Sailing of Mut festival's proximity to the Winter Solstice could present possibilities for a Tameran observance; you could honor Mut's return as the Eye of the Sun, bringing with her an eventual return to longer days.

If you do opt to observe the Sailing of Mut, your offerings, altar setup and ritual structure will closely mirror the Sailing of Hathor's. For those good at research, try to find a translation of the so-called "Crossword Hymn to Mut". Because of Mut's close identification with Sakhmet, you can also adapt the Sakhmet hymns in Chapter 6 and in other rituals from this chapter into hymns to Mut-Sakhmet. To add variety, try incorporating this one as well:

"Hail to You, Sakhmet among the great ones, Lady of the Sky, Mistress of the Two Lands; what you wish is what you do among the gods who are in their shrines. All men are possessed with the awe of You, Lady of Life who is with the Green One." *-from Coffin Text 651*

The Feast of Victory - *Hab Nakhtiu*

Historical background: The temple of Horus at Edfu hosted a fairly unique festival during the middle of the second month of Peret. The Feast of Victory commemorated Horus - in both his aspects as Elder Horus and as Son of Isis - utterly defeating Seth and the *Mosu Badesh*, or Children of Rebellion, for acting against Ra. The festival is best known from Ptolemaic inscriptions, but includes older elements such as the Ritual of the Ten Harpoons, which is also known from the Late Period Salt Papyrus. During the rite Horus cast harpoons one-by-one into an effigy of Seth as a hippopotamus, assisted by Isis and a cast of helper demi-gods. He was serenaded by young women representing the princesses of Upper and Lower Egypt, and grain was fed to a goose symbolizing Geb, the god who endorsed Horus to rule as his grandson. A 'butcher' cut up a 'hippo' cake made of *shat* bread and distributed it to the crowd while execration texts were read. The act of eating the symbolic 'hippo' bread was meant to subdue and consume the dangerous powers of Seth.

Scholars have debated whether the Feast of Victory represented an ancient drama, with actions and dialogue recorded in the Edfu temple reliefs, or just a series of mythical interludes and hymns. Egyptologist H. W. Fairman translated and arranged the texts as a drama entitled *The Triumph of Horus*, which has been performed several times since the 1970's at universities in England, Canada and the United States. Other scholars have disagreed with his conclusions, but recently discovered texts including what appear to be notes or stage directions have supported his basic premise. This would make *The Triumph of Horus* the first Egyptian passion play to be re-enacted in modern times.

Modern observance: Devotees of Seth will probably want to avoid this holiday. However, the Feast of Victory doesn't have to act as a declaration of allegiance "for" or "against" anyone; Seth's negative aspects are certainly execrated in the ritual, but the god Himself still seems to find His followers without any ill effects. If you decide to observe the Feast of Victory, use it as a time to purge negativity from your life. This theme of "out with the bad, in with the good" blends seamlessly into secular New Year's. If the Christmas holiday provides a better time frame for the observance, consider emphasizing Horus' solar associations and thus tying them into the winter solstice. If you can find a way to make a hippo cake, add a little theatrical flair and make it red velvet or strawberry. Alternatively, use cupcakes or gingerbread cookies. Red candles are easiest to find at this time of year; stock up on a few for observances later in the liturgical season.

You will need: Milk, water, food offerings and natron; fresh paper, red pens or markers and red string; a ritual tool for piercing (knife, arrow, etc.); scissors; a means to safely burn paper. Another optional element is red wax.

Altar setup: Horus will take center stage here. Reflecting the Edfu drama, an icon of Isis accompanies him on the altar for this rite. Another appropriate icon to use would be a replica of the famous statue of Tutankhamun standing in a papyrus raft with harpoon held aloft, as it evokes Horus striking the enemies of Ra (see photo). Leave room in your ritual space for the ritual destruction of negative forces, in the form of written or drawn images on paper. If performing the rite indoors, have a place where you can take the sealed paper to burn it, such a fireplace, or else take it outside.

The reading from the Edfu texts describes the familiar Egyptian symbol of a winged sun disk, also called the "Horus of Behdet", and its religious significance. If you can find an image of the winged disk, place it prominently on your altar or in your ritual space.

Closeup of the Nakhtiu *altar, including the icon of Tutankhamun as a harpooner. Author's photo.*

The *Hab Nakhtiu* Rite

(In preparation, perform the necessary purifications for yourself and your altar space. Naturally, the Osirian invocation will be used here, to avoid invoking Seth.)

Candle Rite - As you light your candle(s), say:

"Come in peace, bright Eye of Horus, come in peace.
Receive the light.
The Eye of Horus shines, like Ra in the twin Horizons, and evil hides before it. Receive the light.
The Eye of Horus destroys the enemies of Ra in all of their abodes. Receive the light.
The Eye of Horus comes, and I am purified with it.
Receive the light."

- from the Daily Rite of Amun-Ra, Karnak, and Book of the Dead chapter 137B

Opening Invocation – Ring your sistrum. If part of a group, everyone recites:

"Great and Little Enneads of the Gods!
Lords of Ma'at, United in Ma'at,
Great Ones who reject wrongdoing!
Assemble before the Lord of All,
And turn Your Faces toward me!
My heart is straight, my heart is open,
No darkness is in my heart!"

- *also from Ancient Egyptian Literature vols. II and III*

Invocations to Horus and Isis: *(ring sistrum)*

Iiu im hotep, Horu, neb Behdet.
- Come in peace, Horus, Lord of Behdet.

Iiu im hotep, Horu, Ba Iabty.
- Come in peace, Horus, Soul of the East.

Iiu im hotep, Horu, sab shuty.
- Come in peace, Horus, One of Dappled Plumage.

Iiu im hotep, Horu, notjer a'ah.
- Come in peace, Horus, Greatest God.

Iu em hotep Iset, Uret Hekau.
- Welcome in peace, Isis, Great of Magic.

Iu em hotep Iset, mut Horu.
- Welcome in peace, Isis, Mother of Horus.

Iu em hotep Iset, notjerit a'ah.
- Welcome in peace, Isis, Great Goddess.

Iu em hotep Iset, nebet pet.
- Welcome in peace, Isis, Lady of the Sky.

Offering Rite:
Water: "Take these, Your cool waters that are the Inundation."
Milk: "Milk, milk, may You taste it in Your shrine."
Incense: "I give You incense, I give You incense, great of purity."
Natron: "This is Your natron of Horus, this is Your natron of Djehuty, this is Your natron among the gods'."
Food offering: "Take this, Your bread on which gods live."

Presentation: "Turn Yourselves to these, Your offerings, oh Horus and Isis, on this Your happy day of feast."

Execration, with Recitations from the Edfu Drama and Book of Overthrowing Set:
"Come, let us hasten to the Pool of Horus,
That we may see the Falcon in his ship,
The Son of Isis in His war-galley,
Like Ra in the Bark of the Morning.

Set thought to oppress Him, but Horus shall defeat him."

Binding: Draw a figure of the Set-animal in red on fresh paper. Write the names or qualities of negative forces within the figure. Alternatively, write in red ink on paper the names or qualities of negative forces, then tie them together using red string.

"Oh Horus, guard us from the Evil Ones,
As a wall around a fortress,
As a watchman over His village."

Trampling: Placing the figure on the ground, step on it with the left foot.
"Fall on your face, you rebels,
Son of Nut and his supporters!
Who turned to strife, who returned to rage,
Who mock Him who was placed above you!"

Spearing: Pierce the paper with ritual tool (arrow, spear, etc.).

"The gods of the sky are in terror of Horus.
He takes hold of the harpoon shaft,
For Isis is its Mistress.
She forgets not the night of the flood,
Forgets not the hour of turmoil.

Hold fast, Horus, hold fast!"
[This line was used as an audience response in productions of *The Triumph of Horus*.]

Cutting: Cut the paper up.

"Horus forever holds power
Over Set and the Mosu Badesh.
Their evil turns against them,
Their sins return to them.

Set thought to oppress Him, But Horus has defeated him."
[If doing a group ritual, this line will also serve well for call-and-response.]

Burning: Burn the paper in a fire, or alternatively, seal it with white wax before burning or burying it.

Curse from The Triumph of Horus:
"Be annihilated, Set and your followers, be annihilated!
You shall not exist and your souls shall not exist.
You shall not exist and your bodies shall not exist.
You shall not exist and your children shall not exist.
You shall not exist and your flesh shall not exist.

You shall not exist and your bones shall not exist.
You shall not exist and your magic shall not exist.
You shall not exist and no place where you are shall exist.

Justified is Horu, Lord of Behdet, against Set and the Mosu Badesh.
Justified is Osir, Khenti-Amentiu, against Set and the Mosu Badesh.
Justified are Hathor, Lady of Yunit, and Djehuty, Lord of Khemnu, against their enemies."

(ring sistrum)

Recitation from *The Legend of the Winged Disk*:
"Thereupon Horu of Behdet changed into the Great Winged Disk, and placed Himself upon the bow of the Barque of Ra. And He placed at his sides Nekhebet and Wadjit in the form of uraeus-cobras, so that They would make the Evil Ones to tremble in their limbs. The fiends' brazenness was replaced by fear, they did not rise up, and they died straightaway.

"And Ra-Horakhety said to Djehuty, 'You shall put this Winged Disk in every place where I dwell, and in all the places of the gods of Upper Egypt, and all the places of the gods of Lower Egypt, and in all the Land of Horus, that it may drive away evil."
- from the Edfu texts, updated from Budge's translation in Legends of the Egyptian Gods

Prayer: This is your time for silent prayer, meditation or reflection. Breathe deeply, exhale, and let the energy you've built up slowly release itself.

Closing Invocation: *(ring sistrum)*
"Great and Little Enneads of the Gods!
Great Ones before the Lord of All;
We thank You and wish You well!
Remember me, be where You like, and come again in kindness!"
- also inspired by Osiris hymn, Ancient Egyptian Literature vol. II

To conclude the rite, say: "*In-un-Ma'a*" [Truly it Is]

End of Rite

Feast of Lifting the Sky (or Filling the Sacred Eye)

Historical background: The end of Peret II marked the mid-point of the year on the Egyptian calendar, and this was evidently a special occasion. The Middle Kingdom name for the month was *Rekh Ur*, or "Great Burning", which some believe referred to the mid-year festival; however, records are still too sketchy to decipher anything conclusively prior to the Ptolemaic Era. Mid-year did seem to be an important and solemn occasion, though, as the opening to Chapter 125 of the Book of the Dead refers to 'seeing the Sacred Eye filled on the second month of winter, last day'.

The Feast of Lifting the Sky honored the Creator, whose identity changed by location. Thebes celebrated "Amun in His Lifting the Sky", and nearby Deir el-Medina honored the variant Great Feast of Ptah. In the mythological background to this feast, Ptah took on the role of Shu by separating the sky from the earth. Locals addressed him as "King of the Two Lands", "Gracious of Face" "Who Lifts the Sky With His Hand".

At the Greco-Roman temple at Esna the holiday took on a unique flavor. It honored Khnum, there associated with Ra-Atum and Ptah. His image was taken outside in the morning for an Opening of the Mouth rite and exposure to sunlight in the "Touching of the Sun". Then Khnum's statue was taken to the temple *mammisi*, or birth house, to commemorate his creation of the gods, especially Horus. The gods gave the divine child Horus gifts, then Horus himself addressed them. Women sang songs and played sistrums or hand drums, and the Horus child (probably his icon) was presented to the crowd. The final rite was called the "Transmission of the Wheel to Females", referring to Khnum's potter's wheel. Texts were recited that called for worship of Khnum and the Uraeus goddess, identified with Hathor and Sakhmet as the Eye of Ra. Humankind sprang from the tears of Ra's Eye, as the hymns recalled, thus Hathor and Sakhmet were the mothers of humanity. Finally came the pronouncement that Khnum's Potter's Wheel (which was also an actual sacred object kept in the temple) and its creative power had been transferred into the bodies of all female beings. A prayer was said for Khnum to protect all that was formed in the womb. The rites also called for three young girls who had garlands or ribbons tied on them; one represented a pregnant woman, another her child, and the third represented someone either just born or about to deliver.

Modern observance: How you choose to celebrate this feast will depend on who your patron deities are. You could focus on Ra, Amun, Ptah, or even all three; recall that by the Ramesside era They were often honored as a trinity. Hathor or Sakhmet will also figure prominently in the observance, although Bast could be honored as the Eye of Ra in Her own right. This occasion marks the midpoint in the Egyptian liturgical year, which roughly coincides with secular New Year's. Use it as a time for solemnity, reflection, celebrating what is complete and looking ahead to the rest of the year.

You will need: Milk, water, ritual oil, natron; for food offerings, including something to serve as "five white loaves and five flat loaves" and "roast meat": cookies, bread or donuts and summer sausage have served well. You will also need four white or red candles and an *udjat* image in red or gold.

Altar setup: Center Ra, Amun, Ptah (or all three as applicable) in the altar arrangement, with the Eye Goddess in front of and slightly below them. The *udjat* eye will go either at the feet of the goddess, or if necessary can be used in place of a goddess icon in front of Ra (see the photo following the ritual section). Leave space for offerings in front of the *udjat*.

The Rites of Lifting the Sky and Filling the Sacred Eye

(In preparation, perform the necessary purifications for yourself and your altar space.)

Candle Rite - As you light your candle(s), say:

"Come in peace, bright Eye of Horus, come in peace.
Receive the light.
The Eye of Horus shines, like Ra in the twin Horizons, and evil hides before it. Receive the light.
The Eye of Horus destroys the enemies of Ra in all of their abodes. Receive the light.
The Eye of Horus comes, and I am purified with it.
Receive the light."

- *from the Daily Rite of Amun-Ra, Karnak, and Book of the Dead chapter 137B*

Opening Invocation – Ring your sistrum. If part of a group, everyone recites:

"Great Ennead of the gods who are in Iunu (yoo-NOO)!
Ra, in Your appearance at the First Time;
Ra's Twins, Shu and Tefnut;
Geb and Nut, Lord of Earth and Lady of Heaven;
Osiris [Osir], Isis [Iset], Set and Nephthys [Nebet-Hat];
Turn Your faces toward us!
Behold what is in our innermost;
Our hearts are straight, our hearts are open,
No darkness is in our hearts!"

- *adapted from Osiris hymn of Amunmose and hymn to Hathor in Denderah, Ancient Egyptian Literature vols. II and III*

Invocations to Ra and Ptah: *(This version omits Amun; add His invocations as needed. Begin by ringing your sistrum)*

Iu im hotep Ra, neb Pesdjet.
- Come in peace, Ra, Lord of the Nine.

Iu im hotep Ra, wa en Nun.
- Come in peace, Ra, Unique One of Nun.

Iu im hotep Ra, neb pet.
- Come in peace, Ra, Lord of the Sky.

Iu im hotep Ra, Neb-ir Djer.
- Come in peace, Ra, Lord to the Limit.

Iiu im hotep, Ptah en Ta-Sut Noferu.
- Come in peace, Ptah, of the Beautiful Place.

Iiu im hotep, Ptah, neb Ma'at.
- Come in peace, Ptah, Lord of Truth.

Iiu im hotep, Ptah, Nisut Tawy.
- Come in peace, Ptah, King of the Two Lands.

Iiu im hotep, Ptah, Akh Pet im Hap-ef.
- Come in peace, Ptah, Who Lifts the Sky With His Hand.

Offering Rite:
Water: "Take these, Your cool waters that are the Inundation."
Milk: "Milk, milk, may You taste it in Your shrine."
Incense: "I give You incense, I give You incense, great of purity."
Natron: "This is Your natron of Horus, this is Your natron of Djehuty,
this is Your natron among the gods."
Ointment: "Receive this ointment, from the forehead of Ra."
Food: "Take this, Your bread, on which gods live."

Presentation: Turn Yourself to these, Your offerings, Ra, Lord of the Nine, and Ptah of the Gracious Face, on this Your Feast of Lifting the Sky in Makhir.

(ring sistrum)

Recitation - Filling the Sacred Eye:
"The Mighty One appears, lighting up the Horizon. Atum appears, perfumed with incense, the Luminous One who rises in the sky! The Mansion of the Benben is in joy and all its residents are assembled. A voice calls out within the shrine, a shout reverberates throughout Duat, obeisance is done at the words of Atum-Horakhety. His Majesty gives command to the Ennead attending Him, for He is happy to contemplate the Sacred Eye:

'Behold, my body, to which protection has been given; and all my limbs, which have been made to flourish.'

His Majesty's words go forth, and His Eye rests in Her place upon His brow in the fourth hour of the night, and the land is happy in this last day of Makhir. The Majesty of the Sacred Eye is before the Ennead, Atum shines as on the First Occasion and the Sacred Eye is in His head. Ra-Atum the Everlasting, the Sacred Eye, Shu, Geb, Osir, Set and Horu, Dhejuty who travels Eternity, Nut, Isut, Nebet-hat, Hathor the Victorious, the two *Shemayet* Goddesses, Ma'at, Anupu of the Sacred Land, born of Eternity, and the *Ba* of Djedu; when the Sacred Eye has been filled in the presence of the Lord to the Limit, standing completed and content, these gods are joyful on this day. Their hands support Her and the Feast of all the gods is celebrated. They say:

'Hail to You and praise to Ra! The Sacred Bark sails and A'apep is felled.

'Hail to You and praise to Ra! The form of Khepri has come into being.

'Hail to You and praise to Ra! Rejoice over Him, for His enemies have been driven away.

'Hail to You and praise to Ra! The heads of the *Mosu Badesh* have been cut off.

Worship to You and praise to Ra!'"
- from Book of the Dead Chapter 140

Offering to the Sacred Eye: Place the "five white loaves and five flat loaves" and meat offering on a tray in front of the *Udjat* eye. Light the four candles around the *Udjat* and offer fresh incense. (There is a reason this feast was at one time called the "Great Burning"!)

The readings and instructions from Book of the Dead Chapter 140 stop here, but this would be an ideal point to read from a hymn to Hathor or Sakhmet, or from the Book of Overthrowing A'apep. You can also read from the Hymn to Ptah in Chapter 6. Another good choice would be this adaptation from Coffin Text 80, honoring the god Shu:

"Oh You eight Heh-gods of Heh-gods,
Who encircle the sky with Your arms,
Who gather together sky and earth for Geb,
Shu fashioned You in chaos, in Nun, in darkness and gloom.
He allots to You Geb and Nut,
While Shu is Repeating (*Neheh*) and Tefnut is Enduring (*Djet*).

Shu is the one whom Atum fashioned,
His robe is the air of life.
A cry for Him went out from the mouth of Atum,
The air opened upon His ways.

He makes the sky light after darkness,
His pleasing color is the breath of Atum.
Storm clouds in the sky are His efflux,
Hailstorms and dusk are His sweat.
The length of the sky is His stride,
The width of the earth are His settlements.

All living things upon the back of Geb,
By Atum's command does Shu govern them;
His life is in their nostrils,
He guides breath into their throats."

– *adapted from Raymond O. Faulkner's translation*

(ring sistrum)

Prayer: This can be your time for silent prayer, meditation or reflection. Breathe deeply, exhale, and let the energy you've built up slowly release itself.

Closing Invocation: (*ring sistrum*)

"Great Ennead of the gods in Iunu!
Ra, in Your appearance at the First Time;
Ra's Twins, Shu and Tefnut;
Geb and Nut, Lord of Earth and Lady of Heaven;
Osiris [Osir], Isis [Iset], Set and Nephthys [Nebet-Hat];
I thank You, and wish You well!
Remember me, be where You like, and come again in kindness!
Seneb-ti!"

- *inspired from Osiris hymn of Amunmose*

To conclude the rite, say: "*In-un-Ma'a*" [Truly it Is]

End of Rite

The Sacred Eye at Ra's feet was painted in gold on a piece of lapis lazuli. Author's photo.

Feasts of Min, Rennutet and Khnum

Historical background: Grain that had been sown in early *Peret* was ready to be harvested by the beginning of the next season, *Shomu* (or Summer). Different harvest festivals were celebrated in different regions, all honoring gods of fertility and creative power. One of the better documented feasts celebrated the ithyphallic god Min, and was also called "the Birth of Min". According to reliefs at Medinet Habu, the one-day festival began with Min as an aspect of Osiris who impregnated Isis. After the statue of Min was enthroned and freshly-cut grain was offered to him, he was celebrated as Min-Horus, the "Bull of His Mother".

Elsewhere the cobra-goddess Rennutet was honored. Rennutet (also spelled Renenut or Renenutet) was a maternal patroness of harvest and plenty, said to suckle Nepri, the personification of grain who later assimilated to Osiris. In Deir el-Medina she was identified with Meret-seger. At Esna, Rennutet was honored with Khnum, who was said to have "given birth" to her during the first month of Shomu. Other texts refer to the month, given the name Pa-Khonsu, as the month of "the birth of all the gods".

Modern observance: Many of us live in a temperate climate zone, where March is a time of planting instead of harvest. Traditional school calendars present one aspect of life nearing completion in spring, however, so for students or instructors the theme of things coming to fruition could be quite relevant. Other observers might choose to focus on fertility, abundance, or the birth of patron deities not attributed during the Epagomenal Days or *Upet Ronpet*.

You will need: Milk, water, food offerings, natron; a small bundle of grain, and/or items representing completion that are to be blessed. Optional are red ribbons to wear as fillets symbolizing Min's potency. To make a dais for Min, try painting an overturned wooden tray or box in red or gold color.

Altar setup: Icon statues of the ithyphallic Min are rather difficult to come by, so images of him will have to be either specially commissioned, hand-made or printed and laminated. For the rite given here, Min will be honored in his transformation from Osiris to Horus; since Isis is His counterpart, you may want to include an icon of Her as well. Start the service with Min at the front of the altar and the dais behind Him. He will be placed on the dais as part of the service.

If you prefer instead to focus on Khnum and Rennutet, unfortunately you will have to do some improvising. Rennutet icons are difficult to come by, although Khnum statues are fairly easy to find online. Use your available resources to represent the deities you choose to focus your observance upon, and incorporate your hymns and offerings accordingly.

The Feast of Min Rite

(In preparation, perform the necessary purifications for yourself and your altar space.)

Candle Rite - As you light your candle(s), say:

"Come in peace, bright Eye of Horus, come in peace.
Receive the light.
The Eye of Horus shines, like Ra in the twin Horizons, and evil hides before it. Receive the light.
The Eye of Horus destroys the enemies of Ra in all of their abodes. Receive the light.
The Eye of Horus comes, and I am purified with it.
Receive the light."

- *from the Daily Rite of Amun-Ra, Karnak, and Book of the Dead chapter 137B*

Opening Invocation – Ring your sistrum. If part of a group, everyone recites:

"Great Ennead of the gods who are in Iunu (yoo-NOO)!
Ra, in Your appearance at the First Time;
Ra's Twins, Shu and Tefnut;
Geb and Nut, Lord of Earth and Lady of Heaven;
Osiris [Osir], Isis [Iset], Set and Nephthys [Nebet-Hat];

Turn Your faces toward us!
Behold what is in our innermost;
Our hearts are straight, our hearts are open,
No darkness is in our hearts!"

- *adapted from Osiris hymn of Amunmose and hymn to Hathor in Denderah, Ancient Egyptian Literature vols. II and III*

Invocation to Min: *(ring sistrum)*

Iiu im hotep, Min, qa'i shuty.
- Come in peace, Min, Tall of Plumes.

Iiu im hotep, Min, sa Iset.
- Come in peace, Min, Son of Isis.

Iiu im hotep, Min, Ka Mut-ef.
- Come in peace, Min, Bull of His Mother.

Iiu im hotep, Min, notjer a'ah.
- Come in peace, Min, Greatest God.

Iu em hotep Iset, Uret Hekau.
- Welcome in peace, Isis, Great of Magic.

Iu em hotep Iset, mut Horu.
- Welcome in peace, Isis, Mother of Horus.

Iu em hotep Iset, notjerit a'ah.
- Welcome in peace, Isis, Greatest Goddess.

Iu em hotep Iset, nebet pet.
- Welcome in peace, Isis, Lady of the Sky.

Offering Rite:
Water: "Take these, Your cool waters that are the Inundation."
Milk: "Milk, milk, may You taste it in Your shrine."
Incense: "I give You incense, I give You incense, great of purity."
Natron: "This is Your natron of Horus, this is Your natron of Djehuty, this is Your natron among the gods."
Food: "Take this, Your bread, on which gods live."

Presentation: Turn Yourself to these, Your offerings, oh Min, on this Your day of feast.

(ring sistrum)

Censing the God - Light incense and gently waft the smoke around Min's icon. Read aloud (if using as a group ritual, have participants read different parts):

"Be exalted, Oh Min, my lord!
Arise, Oh Min, my lord,
You are vindicated before Ra-Atum!

Oh She who raises up the land,
The throne of the Great Bull, the throne of the Great Bull,
She is the one whom the Great Bull impregnates.

I am Min, standing on the desert
After He has seized all lands.
He makes you tremble, the outgoing strider,
Youth of the desert, One of Gebju [Coptos]!

Behold me!
As for the Great Bull, as for the Great Bull,
The Great One penetrates into Her."
- from the Medinet Habu texts, United With Eternity

Enthronement of Min - Place His icon onto the dais. Read aloud:

"Hail to You, Oh Min, who impregnates His mother!
You have come forth from the very great door,
You stand upon the dais of Ma'at
And You give commands together with Your father, Osiris."

Offering of the Harvest - Place something finished, or symbolizing something you have finished or wish to see completed, on the altar before Min. If part of a group, have female participants circumambulate the altar seven times, to echo a role once played by the queen.

"Truly, Min has gone to the dais. He has brought to us the hymns that issue from the mouth of His mother, Isis. To us Min has come, strong and powerful! Min is vindicated against His enemies!"

Annunciation of Min-Horus:
"Oh Imsety, Hapy, Duamutef, Qebehsenuef! Go to the South, North, East and West, and tell the gods of the South, North, East and West, that Horus, son of Isis and Osiris, has taken unto Himself the Dual Crown!"
- from the Medinet Habu texts, United With Eternity

At this point, you can also read the Hymn to Min from Chapter 6.
(ring sistrum)

Prayer: This can be your time for silent prayer, meditation or reflection. Breathe deeply, exhale, and let the energy you've built up slowly release itself.

Closing Invocation: *(ring sistrum)*
"Great Ennead of the gods in Iunu!
Ra, in Your appearance at the First Time;
Ra's Twins, Shu and Tefnut;
Geb and Nut, Lord of Earth and Lady of Heaven;
Osiris [Osir], Isis [Iset], Set and Nephthys [Nebet-Hat];
I thank You, and wish You well!
Remember me, be where You like, and come again in kindness!
Seneb-ti!"
- inspired from Osiris hymn of Amunmose

To conclude the rite, say: "*In-un-Ma'a*" [Truly it Is]

End of Rite

Beautiful Feast of the Valley - *Hab Nefer en Pa-Inet*

Historical background: The Feast of the Valley is one of the best-known Theban festivals along with the Opet festival. It generally commenced at the beginning of Shomu II (*Pa'en Inet*). The festival dates back to at least the Middle Kingdom, continued through Greco-Roman times and is still celebrated, albeit in modified form, as the Muslim festival of Al-Haggag. The "Valley" referred to in the original feast name is a wadi in western Thebes that was sacred to Hathor, Lady of the West. Amun, via his icon, travelled across the Nile in procession to commune with Hathor in her sacred conclave. Later in the New Kingdom, the icons of Mut and Khonsu travelled with him, perhaps to emphasize a link between Mut and Hathor. This hallowed ground became the site of Nebhepetra-Montuhotep's temple, Hatshepsut's temple of Deir-el Bahari, and a now-ruined temple of Thutmose III, all meant to receive Amun during his tour of the western valley.

The veil between the living and the dead was believed to be thinnest at that point in the year, and many of the festival observances centered on communing with the blessed dead. Amun, who possessed supreme powers of fertility and renewal, participated with Hathor in re-energizing and giving rebirth to the blessed dead. They were also said to "pour water", *wa'h mu*, for the dead. On the human level, the king would pour water for his royal ancestors and native Thebans would observe much the same rite for their own departed loved ones. Families would hold nocturnal banquets in the chapels of their family tombs, drinking heavily so that they could commune with their dead in Hathor's care. Text references from Deir el-Medina also mention two days of offering to the gods.

Modern observance: The curious combination of fertility and communion with the dead lacks a clear parallel in mainstream Pagan practices. An approach we took one year in our open circle was to celebrate the Feast of the Valley on Memorial Day weekend, tying the commemoration of fallen veterans into a more general memorial of the blessed dead that also anticipated the coming of summer. A more strict Kemetic observance could be held around April 28th, honoring Amun and Hathor. Tamerans could use the occasion for their Beltane Sabbat.

You will need: Milk, water, food offerings, natron, ritual oil, flowers, beer (if available); a vessel for pouring water, a red pot or ceramic plate, and pictures of departed loved ones you might wish to honor. If you lack pictures or tokens of your *akhu* (loved ones), write their names on a sheet of parchment-colored paper or on papyrus, which can be found online.

Altar setup: Center Amun and Hathor in the altar, with flowers and pictures or the names of loved ones around them. Make a space where you can safely smash the red vessel; leave it on the ground inside your ritual space, off of the altar itself.

The *Hab Nefer en Pa-Inet* Rite

(In preparation, perform the necessary purifications for yourself and your altar space.)

Candle Rite - As you light your candle(s), say:

"Come in peace, bright Eye of Horus, come in peace.
Receive the light.
The Eye of Horus shines, like Ra in the twin Horizons, and evil hides before it. Receive the light.
The Eye of Horus destroys the enemies of Ra in all of their abodes. Receive the light.
The Eye of Horus comes, and I am purified with it.
Receive the light."

- *from the Daily Rite of Amun-Ra, Karnak, and Book of the Dead chapter 137B*

Opening Invocation – Ring your sistrum. If part of a group, everyone recites:

"Great and Little Enneads of the Gods!
Lords of Ma'at, United in Ma'at,
Great Ones who reject wrongdoing!
Assemble before the Lord of All,

And turn Your Faces toward me!
My heart is straight, my heart is open,
No darkness is in my heart!”

- *also adapted from Osiris hymn of Amunmose and hymn to Hathor in Denderah, Ancient Egyptian Literature vols. II and III*

Invocations to Amun and Hat-Hor: *(ring sistrum)*

Iiu im hotep, Amun, neb Waset.
- Come in peace, Amun, Lord of Thebes.

Iiu im hoteo, Amun en Khepy Nofer.
- Come in peace, Amun, of the Beautiful Encounter.

Iiu im hotep, Amun, neb neheh.
- Come in peace, Amun, Lord of Eternal Renewal.

Iiu im hotep, Amun, notjer a'ah.
- Come in peace, Amun, Greatest God.

Iiu im hotep, Hat-Hor, nebet Amentet.
- Come in peace, Hathor, Lady of the West.

Iiu im hotep, Hat-Hor, nebet pa'Inet.
- Come in peace, Hathor, Lady of the Valley.

Iiu im hotep, Hat-Hor, nebet pet.
- Come in peace, Hathor, Mistress of the Sky.

Iiu im hotep, Hat-Hor, notjerit a'ah.
- Come in peace, Hathor, Greatest Goddess.

Offering Rite:

Water: "Take these, Your cool waters that are the Inundation."
Milk: "Milk, milk, may You taste it in Your shrine."
Incense: "I give You incense, I give You incense, great of purity."

Natron: "This is Your natron of Horus, this is Your natron of Djehuty, this is Your natron among the gods."
Ointment: "Receive this ointment, from the forehead of Ra."
Food: "Take this, Your bread, on which gods live."
Flowers: "Take these flowers, that they may refresh You."
Beer: "Receive this beer that is pleasing to Your hearts on this, Your feast of the Desert Valley."

Presentation: Turn Yourself to these, Your offerings, Great Amun and Lady Hat-Hor, and receive them from me; may Your hearts take joy in them.

Wa'h Mu (Offering Water to the Deceased):
LIBATION:
Osir, take unto Yourself all those who speak ill of their names.
Djehuty, go, take the enemies of these Blessed Dead on behalf of Osir.

RECITE FOUR TIMES: Do not let loose of them, beware not to let loose of them.

INCENSE:
Someone has gone to be with his ka;
Osiris has gone to be with his ka;
Seth has gone to be with his ka;
Horus, Looking Forward, has gone to be with his ka;
__*read from list*__ have gone to be with their kas.

Come, you Blessed Dead! Someone has come, you shall not need;
The Lady of the West has come, and you shall not need;
Hathor has come, and you shall not need.
Your purity is that of the gods who have gone, but not withdrawn from us.

Raise yourselves to this fresh water and to this incense that I have given you. You have been purified for the feast days like the Unwearying One of Abydos.

- *adapted from Pyramid Texts 23, 25 and 32*

Voice Offering:

Peret kheru, ta, heneket, kha khau, apdu, senotjer, merhat, khut nebet nofret wabet ankhet notjer im, en kau en...[read from your list of loved ones, or name them in turn]*...ma'a-kheru her notjer a'ah.*

"A voice offering of bread, beer, a thousand of beef and poultry, incense and oil, and all good and pure things on which a god lives, for the *ka*s of _______, true of voice before the Great God."

(ring sistrum)

Smashing of the Plate:
"This is the sound Eye of Horus; it has been set for you so that you may grow strong, and that evil may be afraid of you."

– *from Pyramid Text 244*

(smash plate)

Hymn to Amun: *(ring sistrum)*

O Amun, heaven is uplifted for You,
Ground is trodden for You.
Ptah with His two hands makes a chapel
As a resting place for Your heart!

How great is Amun, beloved god!
He rises in Karnak, His city, Lord of Life!
The beautiful face of Amun, beloved power,
Whom the gods love to behold,
Mighty One who came from the horizon!
All of Amun's domain is in feast.
Happy it is for Amun-Ra,
The One whom mankind loves!
- *adapted from the tomb of Aahmose, The Life of Meresamun*

You can also read from the Egyptian-language Hymn to Amun-Ra, or the Hymn to Hathor, both found in Chapter 6.

(ring sistrum)

Prayer: This can be your time for silent prayer, meditation or reflection. Breathe deeply, exhale, and let the energy you've built up slowly release itself.

Closing Invocation: *(ring sistrum)*
"Great and Little Enneads of the Gods!
Great Ones before the Lord of All;
We thank You and wish You well!
Remember me, be where You like, and come again in kindness!"
- also inspired by Osiris hymn, Ancient Egyptian Literature vol. II

To conclude the rite, say: "*In-un-Ma'a*" [Truly it Is]

End of Rite

For this Feast of the Valley altar, laminated art of Amun and Hathor served for the icon. Author's photo.

The Esna Feasts and Feast of Neith

Historical background: Also occurring in early Shomu II (*Pa'en-Inet*), the first Esna feast celebrated the Myth of Destruction of Mankind, but with a twist - in their version, Ra abdicated his rule over Creation and hid, leaving Shu to destroy the forces of chaos. The icon of Khnum, acting as Ra, travelled to hide in the northern temple building known as the House of the God. Participants playing the rebels "found" Khnum's hiding place, and inside priests turned the icon to face away from his shrine door to signify that he was in hiding. Outside, men and priests would make a great noise until about noon, after which the icon was taken in procession south again to the House of Khnum.

A similar but better-documented feast took place in late Shomu III *(Apip)*. Khnum travelled in procession to another temple area by the sacred lake, referred to as Red Lake. There he stayed overnight, and the only lights allowed were to be inside the temple. No singing or musical accompaniment was performed. The next day wrapped up the "Festival of Taking Up the Club" with a mock battle by the lake. It was apparently similar to an event described elsewhere by Herodotus, in which men 'with vows to perform' set upon each other with clubs. Such mock battles find a parallel in a Central American festival meant to protect the world from chaos; the men beat each other quite bloody, but have no hard feelings toward each other afterward!

Another major festival on the Esna calendar was the Feast of Neith, which took place during mid-*Apip*. In the story celebrated during the feast, Neith was identified with the primeval goddess *Mehet-Uret*, or "Great Flood", who took the form of a cow. By lifting Ra upon her horns, she kept him above the crocodile-infested waters; appropriate, as Neith was also the mother of the crocodile god Sobek. Within the temple precincts at Esna, priests carried her icon statue into an open-air courtyard so she could reunite with Ra's sunlight. Lining up into two rows, the priests were ritually purified with water before taking Neith's statue on a public procession, heralded by much feasting and singing.

Modern observance: Attempting either of the three Esna feasts would require a great deal of improvisation. Solitary Egyptian

Pagans would not be able to re-create the Festival of Taking Up the Club – and a group may not want to go that far, either! Those who venerate Khnum could commemorate His aspect as Khnum-Ra, and Shu as His defender. Neith can also be celebrated as both protector of Ra and Mother Goddess; use Her titles in Appendix A to build your own prayers and invocations. If celebrating with a group, instead of mock combat you could consider a less physical contest, ranging from a ball game to a senet (Egyptian board game, available in various versions online) match-off to video games. May the forces of Shu win!

Beautiful Feast of the Reunion - Hab Nefer en Sekhen

Historical background: At Denderah, home temple of Hathor, the Feast of the Reunion began around Denit, or First Quarter (which is actually a half-moon). Hathor's icon was loaded onto a portable bark shrine, then onto an actual barge in order to sail upstream to Edfu for a conjugal visit with Horus. Accompanied by a cadre of priests, officials and pilgrims, Hathor arrived in Edfu amid much celebration. Offerings of myrrh, aromatics and sistrums were presented to Hathor amid hymns encouraging her to "unite with He of Dappled Plumage", being Horus. Aside from the fertility associations, though, the Reunion Feast also bore harvest-related elements. Cattle or perhaps four calves were driven to symbolically thresh grain, offerings were made to the "divine ancestors" and on the second day of the feast four geese were released to bear the news that Horus had received the Red and White Crowns. Execration rites were also performed, including one where enemies of the state were represented by a red wax hippopotamus that was ritually mutilated.

When the Edfu festivities drew to a close, Hathor travelled back to Denderah to symbolically give birth to her and Horus' child. At Edfu the child was celebrated as Horus-Sema-Tawy (Harsomtus in Greek), while at Edfu he was known as Ihy, the naked sistrum player who was sometimes identified with Khonsu.

Modern observance: Kemetic Pagans celebrate love and marriage during the Feast of the Reunion. Its relative proximity in date to the fertility-themed Midsummer festival suggests a ready adaptation for Tameran Wiccans. As Hathor is patroness of love, women, children and family life, the Reunion Feast would be an excellent time for handfastings or weddings; or for those seeking a partner to invoke the aid of the "Golden One". The celebration does not have to be entirely centered around the feminine mystique, however. Horus is celebrated as king to Hathor's queen.

You will need: Milk, water, food offerings, natron, ritual oil, beer (if available); myrrh, incense and sistrums. Optional is a red pot for execration rites.

Altar setup: Horus and Hathor share space on the altar, with room for offerings in front of them. Try to incorporate flowers into the altar decorations. If you will be performing an execration, keep your red pot on the ground in front of the altar.

The *Hab Nefer en Sekhen* Rite

(In preparation, perform the necessary purifications for yourself and your altar space.)

Candle Rite - As you light your candle(s), say:

"Come in peace, bright Eye of Horus, come in peace.
Receive the light.
The Eye of Horus shines, like Ra in the twin Horizons, and evil hides before it. Receive the light.
The Eye of Horus destroys the enemies of Ra in all of their abodes. Receive the light.
The Eye of Horus comes, and I am purified with it.
Receive the light."

- *from the Daily Rite of Amun-Ra, Karnak, and Book of the Dead chapter 137B*

Opening Invocation – Ring your sistrum. If part of a group, everyone recites:

"Great and Little Enneads of the Gods!
Lords of Ma'at, United in Ma'at,
Great Ones who reject wrongdoing!
Assemble before the Lord of All,
And turn Your Faces toward me!
My heart is straight, my heart is open,
No darkness is in my heart!"

- *also adapted from Osiris hymn of Amunmose and hymn to Hathor in Denderah, Ancient Egyptian Literature vols. II and III*

Invocations to Horus and Hathor: *(ring sistrum)*

Iiu im hotep, Horu, neb Behdet.
- Come in peace, Horus, Lord of Behdet.

Iiu im hotep, Horu, Ba Iabty. -
Come in peace, Horus, Soul of the East.

Iiu im hotep, Horu, sab shuty.
- Come in peace, Horus, One of Dappled Plumage.

Iiu im hotep, Horu, notjer a'ah.
- Come in peace, Horus, Greatest God.

Iiu im hotep, Hat-Hor, nebet Yunit.
- Come in peace, Hathor, Mistress of Denderah.

Iiu im hotep, Hat-Hor, nebet nub.
- Come in peace, Hathor, Mistress of Gold.

Iiu im hotep, Hat-Hor, notjerit a'ah.
- Come in peace, Hathor, Greatest Goddess.

Iiu im hotep, Hat-Hor, nebet pet.
– Come in peace, Hathor, Mistress of the Sky.

Offering Rite: *(ring sistrum)*
Water: "Take these, Your cool waters that are the Inundation."
Milk: "Milk, milk, may You taste it in Your shrine."
Incense: "I give You incense, I give You incense, great of purity."
Natron: "This is Your natron of Horus, this is Your natron of Djehuty, this is Your natron among the gods."

Ointment: "Receive this ointment, from the forehead of Ra."
Food: "Take this, Your bread, on which gods live."
Beer: "Receive this beer that is pleasing to Your hearts on this, Your beautiful Reunion."

Reversion: Turn Yourself to these, Your offerings, Hat-Hor and Horu, and receive them from me; may Your hearts take joy in them.
(ring sistrum)

Voice Offering:

Peret kheru, ta, heneket, kha khau, apdu, senotjer, merhat, khut nebet nofret wabet ankhet notjer im, en kau en... [read from your list of loved ones, or name them in turn]*...ma'a-kheru her notjer a'ah.*

"A voice offering of bread, beer, a thousand of beef and poultry, incense and oil, and all good and pure things on which a god lives, for the *ka*s of _______, true of voice before the Great God."

(ring sistrum)

Censing of Hathor:
"Oh Powerful One on the throne of Edfu, Who comes down to earth at the smell of incense, Hathor, Great One, Mistress of Yunit! May You be joyful with this finest myrrh, With pleasing fragrance and perfect body, May You be glad and join with He of Dappled Plumage!"
- adapted from Edfu texts

Offering the Sistrum: *(ring sistrum)*
Your sistrum for You,
Oh Mighty One,
Great Flame, Oh Shining One,
The sistrum to quench Your ire.
- adapted from Edfu relief texts

Some Kemetic groups observing this feast read from the New Kingdom love poetry during their Reunion rites. If you choose to do so, many love songs that mention Hathor can be found in Ancient Egyptian Literature vol. II by Miriam Lichtheim.

Four Annunciations of Horus:

Hail, Duamutef, Lord of the East!
Horus is crowned, Lord of Nekhen! *(ring sistrum)*

Hail, Qebehsenuef, Lord of the West!
Horus is crowned, Lord of Upper Egypt! (*ring sistrum)*

Hail, Hapy, Lord of the North!
Horus is crowned, Lord of Pe (PAY)! *(ring sistrum)*

Hail, Imsety, Lord of the South!
Horus is crowned, Lord of Lower Egypt! *(ring sistrum)*

At this point, you can perform an execration as covered in Chapter 5, recite the Hymn to Hathor from Chapter 6, or one of your own.

(ring sistrum)

Prayer: This can be your time for silent prayer, meditation or reflection. Breathe deeply, exhale, and let the energy you've built up slowly release itself.

Closing Invocation: *(ring sistrum)*

"Great and Little Enneads of the Gods!
Great Ones before the Lord of All;
We thank You and wish You well!
Remember me, be where You like, and come again in kindness!"

- also inspired by Osiris hymn, Ancient Egyptian Literature vol. II

To conclude the rite, say: "*In-un-Ma'a*" [Truly it Is]

End of Rite

Feast of Apip

Historical background: During the Middle Kingdom, the month of this feast was called *Ipet-Hemet*, which became *Apip* by the late New Kingdom. It seems to refer to the hippo goddess Tawret, who has been identified as the goddess Ipy (or Aipip) from the Pyramid Texts. How specifically Taweret/Ipy was honored is unknown, though Deir el-Medina accounts refer to Amun of Karnak appearing in procession.

Modern observance: This would have to be a completely improvised rite, as no surviving texts are known detailing the feast. As Taweret was a protectress of children and mothers, this would be the ideal time for groups or Solitary parents to celebrate a children's feast.

New Year's Eve - *Iri Mosyt*

Historical background: The last day of the year, this occasion was also called the "Day of Doing *Mosyt*" (*Iri Mosyt*). At the time of the evening meal, which was probably at sundown, torches were lit. A son or daughter would 'do *mosyt*' by performing rites for the dead. The Cairo Calendar seems to echo the practice by stating that on the last day of the year people should "sing and make offerings".

Modern observance: Egyptian New Year's Eve would not be as raucous as secular New Year's Eve, since five intercalary days follow it instead of New Year's Day. Rather, this is a solemn time to reflect on the end of the year, remember loved ones who have passed and pray for good luck in the coming year. It marks a time of introspection and anticipation.

You will need: Milk, water, food offerings, wine, and a tall white candle as for the *Heriu Diu*, which will commence the following day.

Altar setup: Your *akhu* (departed loved ones) will be the focus. Place pictures or other tokens of them at the forefront; alternatively, make a list of your loved ones' names on papyrus or parchment-colored paper. Light your tall candle(s) to one or either side.

The *Iri Mosyt* Rite

(In preparation, perform the necessary purifications for yourself and your altar space. This rite does not use the customary food offerings, as the focus is upon water and invocation offerings to the deceased.)

Candle Rite - As you light your candle(s), say:

"Come in peace, bright Eye of Horus, come in peace.
Receive the light.
The Eye of Horus shines, like Ra in the twin Horizons, and evil hides before it. Receive the light.
The Eye of Horus destroys the enemies of Ra in all of their abodes. Receive the light.
The Eye of Horus comes, and I am purified with it.
Receive the light."

- *from the Daily Rite of Amun-Ra, Karnak, and Book of the Dead chapter 137B*

Opening Invocation – Ring your sistrum. If part of a group, everyone recites:

"Great and Little Enneads of the Gods!
Lords of Ma'at, United in Ma'at,
Great Ones who reject wrongdoing!
Assemble before the Lord of All,
And turn Your Faces toward me!
My heart is straight, my heart is open,
No darkness is in my heart!"

- *also adapted from Osiris hymn of Amunmose and hymn to Hathor in Denderah, Ancient Egyptian Literature vols. II and III*

Wa'h Mu (Offering Water to the Deceased):

LIBATION:
Osir, take unto Yourself all those who speak ill of their names.
Djehuty, go, take the enemies of these Blessed Dead on behalf of Osir.

RECITE FOUR TIMES: Do not let loose of them, beware not to let loose of them.

INCENSE:
Someone has gone to be with his ka;
Osiris has gone to be with his ka;
Seth has gone to be with his ka;
Horus, Looking Forward, has gone to be with his ka;
__*read from list*__ have gone to be with their kas.

Come, you Blessed Dead! Someone has come, you shall not need;
The Lady of the Sky has come, and you shall not need;
Nut has come, and you shall not need.
Your purity is that of the gods who have gone, but not withdrawn from us.

Raise yourselves to this fresh water and to this incense that I have given you. You have been purified for the feast days like the Unwearying One of Abydos.
- adapted from Pyramid Texts 23, 25 and 32

(ring sistrum)

Recitation for the *Akhu*: (Replace the letter *N* with the names of the *akhu* being honored.)

For Letting a Man Have Quiet By Night, and Everything Customarily Given Him in the Great Mosyt Festival and the Wa'g Festival.
"Lo, *N*! Sky and earth are opened for you, the great gates are opened for you, the gates of the people are thrown open for you, Geb, chiefest of the Gods, has opened His jaws for you.
Lo, *N*! The Ram conducts you to His altars, Soped is keen for you.
Lo, *N*! They remove the dimness of your sight and the wrinkles on your limbs; they open your blind eyes and extend your curled fingers.
Lo, *N*, they open your mouth for you.
Lo, *N*! Lift yourself up on your left side, place yourself upon your right side!
Lo, *N*! Eat your portion, this pure bread which is given, the loaves of this great god whose name is unknown.

Lo, *N*! Drink this pure water which issues from the table, for that Ram has given to you what is his.
Lo, *N*! Ptah-South-of-His-Wall and Sokar have granted you an appearance in the *henu* bark of Geb, chiefest of the Gods.
Lo, *N*! May you go forth by day and by night, may you eat bread and drink beer, may you receive the voice-offerings that are yours.
Come, oh voice offerings!" *(said four times)*
- from Coffin Text 226

Voice Offering:

Peret kheru, ta, heneket, kha khau, apdu, senotjer, merhat, khut nebet nofret wabet ankhet notjer im, en kau en...[read from your list of loved ones, or name them in turn]*...ma'a-kheru her notjer a'ah.*

"A voice offering of bread, beer, a thousand of beef and poultry, incense and oil, and all good and pure things on which a god lives, for the *ka*s of _______, true of voice before the Great God."

(ring sistrum)

Prayer: This can be your time for silent prayer, meditation or reflection. Breathe deeply, exhale, and let the energy you've built up slowly release itself.

Closing Invocation: *(ring sistrum)*

"Great and Little Enneads of the Gods!
Great Ones before the Lord of All;
We thank You and wish You well!
Remember me, be where You like, and come again in kindness!"
- also inspired by Osiris hymn, Ancient Egyptian Literature vol. II

To conclude the rite, say: "*In-un-Ma'a*" [Truly it Is]

End of Rite

Toward Building a Community

Today a newcomer to the Neo-Pagan scene could probably find at least one Wiccan coven in virtually any mid-sized city in America. But perhaps owing to their more specialized nature, practicing Egyptian Pagans tend to be most concentrated in major metropolitan areas. At present, a solitary Tameran or Kemetic would have to travel to either the West Coast, Chicago or Dallas-Fort Worth to find active, "in-person" groups. (Afrocentric Kemetic groups tend to center more in the East Coast, Chicago and Atlanta.) But Egyptian Pagans living outside these hubs of activity face three alternatives: remain Solitaries or "Indie Kemetics"; look online for a forum or group to join; or try to start their own group. Each option has its own merits and disadvantages.

Staying an Independent has the obvious downside of being a sometimes lonely path. Participating in open circles of Wiccans or general Pagan groups can potentially lead an ardent Egyptian Pagan to feel like the "token" group member. Books on Egyptian Paganism still tend to cater to groups, especially Tameran covens, but this book in particular aims to reverse that trend. For all its disadvantages, though, remaining Solitary offers a decided advantage in avoiding the drama and politics that come with any group of people. Besides, if you perform your own rituals by yourself, who's going to tell you that you're "doing it wrong"? For anyone coming out of a group who might have had a bad experience, solitary practice can also offer an excellent chance to re-focus and reflect, especially before deciding to join a different group.

As described above, Egyptian Pagans not living in one of the top metropolitan areas would have to look online in order to participate in a group. The most readily obvious advantage to online groups is their ease of participation; anyone can log in from anywhere in the world. Online groups' most obvious disadvantage is that, like any other Internet-based community, they often have more than their fair share of 'teh dramaz'. Groups that have both online and brick-and-mortar locations may also have different cultures online versus 'in real life'; social dynamics in an Internet forum can easily become something else entirely when people are physically present with one another.

As mercantile as it might sound, when looking for a religious group to potentially join, remember that you are a consumer. You have a right to shop around and compare values before agreeing to invest your time and energies with any group, whether in-person or online. The more you try to find out about an Egyptian Pagan or Kemetic group - or any other group, for that matter - before joining, the more empowered your decision will be. Don't hesitate to ask direct questions in forums. Pay attention to *how* those questions get answered, and not just with *what* kind of answer. Evasive, rote or misleading answers should send up red flags. Pay attention to group dynamics in the forum. Is there a difference between what "insiders" and "outsiders", or "newbies", are allowed to know? Do people "practice what they preach"; meaning, their conduct in the forum matches what their group espouses? Does anyone make you uncomfortable participating in forum discussions? Is there an obvious hierarchy? An unstated hierarchy, or 'cliques' within the group? Can you talk to ex-members? What do they think of the group, and why did they leave? If there are differences between the group's philosophy and your own, or their interpretation of Kemeticism or Paganism and your own, are you comfortable with those differences? These are all important things to consider when checking out any online group. *Never* let the desire to 'belong' to something override your own misgivings or intuition.

"Conning" - No, Not *That* Kind

If you're an Independent Pagan and want to get a feel for other Egyptian Pagans in person, one useful but underrated option is to attend a convention or festival. Much like science-fiction and Japanese anime conventions, Pagan festivals have been occurring in various parts of the country for the past three decades, with new ones emerging every year. While many long-running festivals are held outdoors in rural settings, others are styled more like mainstream conventions and take place in hotels or other urban environs. Some are sponsored by specific groups or covens; others are not. While at present, not many Pagan gatherings boast large presences of Egyptian Pagans - two notable exceptions would be Pantheacon in San Jose and Isis Oasis Convocation in northern California - newer events are actively seeking Egyptian Pagan presenters and participants. These could present great opportunities to meet and network with fellow Egyptian Pagans. Lists of upcoming conventions can be found in magazines, such as *PanGaia* or *Witches and Pagans*; online forums such as The Witches' Voice; or in ads at local alternative shops. Keep in mind that no list is exhaustive, however. Events may be well-advertised in one source but completely omitted in another.

Developing Your "Convention Ninja" Skills

So you've found out about a Pagan Festival or convention that you'd like to attend. You've started to save up some spending money, preregistered if the event requires it, and cleared your calendar so you can travel there and back. That's all you need to prepare...right? Hardly. Convention-going is something of an art, such that seasoned attendees have been known to jokingly call themselves "convention ninjas". Poor planning on an attendee's part can make for an unhappy convention experience, even if the event itself was well-organized and had a variety of activities to offer. By contrast, the well-prepared attendee can have a great time at a modest event, and even contribute to a great experience for fellow con-goers. Many advertised convention guests started out as regular attendees who participated in certain activities or panels year after year.

If you're planning to attend a Pagan festival or convention, these pointers will prove invaluable toward making your experience fun, rewarding, and worth repeating in future years:

Research the area beforehand. Is it in a hotel? If so, how close is it to places to eat, bus lines, the airport, and so on? If it's a camping festival, where is the nearest town? Do they have campsites you can reserve? What will the weather be like that time of year? (This can apply for hotel-based events as well - you won't be spending all of your time indoors!) Even if you won't be driving to the event, knowing the general layout of the area will help you find your way and get to food more easily; some hotels don't have restaurants, or their food services are prohibitively expensive and cease operations long before you've called it a night. Besides, nothing builds new friendships quite like walking as a group to the nearest restaurant for a bite to eat between convention events.

People with disabilities will especially need to investigate thc convention or festival setting beforehand. Unfortunately, most outdoor Pagan festivals are not wheelchair-accessible as yet, which limits the potential attendee's possibilities. Sometimes convention hotels do not have adequate accommodations, so call the hotel staff beforehand and ask specific questions about what you need. Be insistent if nobody seems to know. If all else fails, look for hotels nearby that have better accommodations.

If at all possible, travel with a friend. One clear advantage of travelling with one or more friends is that you can split travel and lodging costs. Conventions are famous (or perhaps infamous?) for hotel rooms crammed with sleeping bags! Having someone you know travelling with you can be both a source of familiarity and safety in a foreign environment. It also allows you and your friend(s) a chance to compare notes after the event is over: what did you both like about it? Dislike? Did anything in particular about the event strike you as odd, either positively or negatively? Would you both look forward to going again next year? If so, is there anything else that either of you might want to bring, or do differently? If you have a friend who is not Egyptian Pagan or even Pagan at all, but still 'hip' enough to travel along with you, that person could offer a great sounding board during and after the festival. As an unattached outsider, they could see issues or possibilities that those of us embedded in the 'Pagan scene' might miss.

If someone else will be reserving your hotel room, know their legal name and travel itinerary. While at first this may seem like obvious advice, even veteran convention-goers have been guilty of ignoring it to their detriment. To give an example: a former friend of mine had planned to meet several friends from an online role-playing game (RPG) at a convention many years ago. One of those RPG friends had booked a hotel room and invited her to join them. Unfortunately, nobody knew anyone else's real name, only their online player names. By the time she arrived in the area, it was late in the evening and no one was available to meet her or show her to the group's hotel room. She ended up booking a hotel room in another part of town, which set a negative tone for the rest of that convention.

Former Friend might be forgiven for not bothering to verify real names or itineraries, as this was some years before September 11th and even before cell phones had become widespread. Today's attendee lacks that excuse. The friend you know from an online forum as Imhotep or Lady Bast will have to have a legal name and contact information in order to book a hotel room for the group, so make sure you know these things before setting out to the convention. If they are reticent to share that information, you should probably consider sharing a room with someone else.

If you travel off-site with anyone, make sure you have alternate means to get back. Some events take place in more than one location. Or at a rural festival, you might go along with a group of people heading off-site for an errand. If you don't drive yourself, make that sure you have more than one way to get back to where you're staying. Keep cab fare on hand if needs be. Especially if a gathering hosts events outside their main venue, you don't want to get stuck at a ritual or activity that gets boring, or even makes you uncomfortable, because you're dependent on another participant for a ride back to your hotel or campsite. This can especially be true if alcohol is involved with any activities, sanctioned or otherwise; in another example, my younger brother rode with friends to a regional ROTC conference… surely a bastion of conservative, upstanding behavior, right? His friends got so drunk the last night of the convention that he quickly grew concerned they would be unable to manage the seven-hour drive home safely. Guess who ended up driving there pick him up? The worst part was that, as we left the hotel, we spotted the bus station about two blocks away! He could have saved us all a great deal of trouble had he kept a cool head, planned alternate possibilities for getting around, and followed the next tip:

Set aside money strictly for your trip home. Speaking as a veteran convention dealer, I have lost count of how many attendees I've seen who spent exuberantly on souvenirs, then had to borrow gas money or bus fare from friends just to get home. Allow yourself a decent budget for souvenirs, certainly, but also give yourself a food budget and a separate reserve that is strictly for your trip home. No matter how tempting that last souvenir is or how insistently coven or group members clamor for donations to their cause of the moment, do not touch your return travel money. Even if you will be taking a bus or plane and your ticket is already covered, that reserve can be put toward unexpected emergencies. (Airport parking fees can be exorbitant.) We dealers would love for you to spend money with us, naturally, but more than that we want you to enjoy the convention and see us again next year.

These words of wisdom may seem simplistic, but in the midst of excitement and euphoria that come with the convention or festival experience, they become easy to forget. Being at a con can feel like being in another world. This can be tremendously fun, but some people get swept up in it. I've known of attendees who tried to subsist on Mountain Dew and M&M's for an entire weekend, passed out because they never went to sleep, or went for an entire four-day weekend without bathing (giving rise to the term, "con funk"!). Conventions share commonalities across genres, but at a religiously-themed gathering in particular, staying 'grounded' is vital to one's sanity. Enjoy the rituals and events, but remember that the normality in between is what gives them their flavor and specialness.

Starting Your Own Group

The third option for Tamerans or Kemetics looking to share their practice is to start a group of their own. This option is the most daunting because it requires a great deal of time, effort and patience; it involves working with other people and learning to compromise. Comparatively few have succeeded in establishing successful Kemetic or Tameran groups thus far, but as the Egyptian Pagan movement continues to grow, more people will eventually take that first step. The rest of this chapter is meant to offer helpful starting points for those enterprising souls.

Networking with other Pagans who share your interest is the first step. Online presents one obvious venue for finding people in your area, through social networking sites like Facebook or MySpace (or the more specific PaganSpace); another excellent source with a local search function is The Witches' Voice, a.k.a. "witchvox". But don't forget local alternative stores, Unitarian Universalist churches and New Age fairs. You can also search online to see if your area has a Pagan Night Out, in which local Pagans meet once a month at a public place – usually a restaurant or bookstore – so that they can get to know each other in a safe and neutral environment. If your area doesn't have one, consider starting one. If you go with a restaurant, choose a location where people who attend can eat inexpensively, preferably in a party room. You don't have to tell the restaurant staff the *exact* nature of your group, unless you know with certainty that they are Pagan-friendly, but make sure that they know ahead of time to reserve a party room on the set date and time of your meet-up. Some other area Pagans and I actually started a monthly meeting at a local Greek and Lebanese restaurant; it got to the point where the owner, a witty and agnostic Palestinian gentleman, would often text me beforehand to verify that we were coming!

Be prepared for the possibility that you may get to know other Pagans in your area and still not have enough shared interest or cohesion to start a practicing Egyptian group. Some Pagans simply do not have the same enthusiasm for focusing on a specific pantheon, especially a non-European one. I've hosted several Egyptian festival rites where area Pagans attended, and the only thing some of them remembered about the rituals was that we smashed plates! If something like this happens, it may not be time for a group yet. Be patient and keep developing your own practice. When you and your future group-mates are ready, you will find each other.

When this *does* finally happen, and you get to the point of discussing building a group or coven, establishing a clear framework at the beginning will go a long way toward future stability. Everyone should have input; when people feel that they have contributed to a collaborative effort, they feel a sense of pride and belonging in it. Conversely, members who feel left out of the process will not be motivated to stay.

One of the best guides on group building is <u>Coven Craft</u> by Amber K. It focuses on mainstream Wicca, but its advice and information can easily be applied to building a Tameran Wiccan, Kemetic Reconstructionist or other Egyptian-themed congregation. It includes information on legal incorporation, managing group resources and dealing with various types of personalities. Just skip over the section on the history of covens, as it draws a bit too heavily from Murray's The Witch-Cult in Western Europe, to get to the important details.

Below are some other helpful questions to ask of your fellow Egyptian Pagans as you begin the process of building a group:

1. What will you adopt as your "group tradition"?
    a. How does your group interpret the Divine? Is it "hard polytheist", henotheist, or other?
    b. Who will your group's primary Gods or Goddesses be?
    c. Will a particular Creation story or other myth be part of your group's tradition?

2. What will your group consider "basic knowledge" that you can teach to members?
    a. Are there certain altar setups, ritual styles or vestments your group wants to adopt? If so, what are their significances? What, if any, correspondences will your group recognize (such as colors, symbolism, etc.)?
    b. What holidays will your group observe? Rites of passage?

3. How will your group be structured?
    a. Will there be specific levels of membership or priesthood? How would they be defined or attained?
    b. Will your group have a code of ethics?
    c. How will your group handle disputes or misconduct? Who will arbitrate in the event of a dispute?
    d. Will your group adopt a charter? If so, what will be the process of emending or adding to that group charter? Who can vote?
    e. How would your group handle potentially divisive issues? What moral decisions are to be left to the individual?

As unpleasant as the topic may seem, establishing a protocol for handling potential disputes is extremely important. Too many groups have been torn apart by a lack of clear boundaries, particularly with regard to sexual behavior, or a lack of consistency in how rules are enforced. One hallmark of toxic groups is an absence of mediation, or means for members to address grievances. By deciding on specifics of how your group will handle disagreements, disputes or misconduct, you will not eliminate *all* potential conflict, but you will mitigate a great deal of drama that could possibly scar the entire group.

In defining group or coven tradition, one more potential pitfall to avoid is inventing too many trappings that are "group-specific": such as jargon, gestures and mannerism, ritual or non-ritual garb, and so on. While every group naturally wants to define its own uniqueness, too much can mentally isolate members from the world around them. The object of establishing a group tradition is not to regulate the lives and practices of individual members, nor to separate everyone from the rest of society, but rather to give everyone a shared framework for group practice.

The startup work of coven- or congregation-building can be the hardest part, but a solid foundation is essential to any construction, physical or metaphorical. Once you've gotten that part down, your first observances together will truly feel like a celebration. What follows is a sample initiation rite that you can use or adapt for your own group.

A Group Initiation Rite

Preparation:

All participants shave and bathe beforehand according to typical practice; fasting is optional. Initiate(s) put on their ceremonial garb prior to the rite.

Officiants set up the altar as needed; light the candles, ring sistrums (or sound other instruments) to begin.

1. Announcing the Initiate(s)

Officiant: "On behalf of Geb, at the fore of the Ennead, and Djehuty, True Scribe of the Ennead, we welcome ________, who is (are) about to become ________ [members, *shemsu*, priest, etc.]."

Group: "Come in peace, _________, come in peace."

2. Purification

Officiant: "What have you to declare?"

Initiate: "I have come before the Gods, with no evil in me and no wrong in me. I live in truth, doing what men ask and the Gods love. I am pure, front, back and middle, and no part of me is empty of truth." *- adapted from Book of the Dead Chapter 125*

Officiant anoints the initiate's head and hands with water from a vase (a blue or gold vase is ideal, but not absolutely essential).

Officiant: "You are pure, you are pure, you are pure, you are pure."

3. Eating Bread

Perform an *Iru* or standard offering for your tradition. Be sure to involve both officiants and initiates in making the offerings. For the Reversion, the officiant holds up the bread, cakes or other food items.

Officiant: "Of what shall you eat?"

Initiate: "I shall eat the bread which Renenutet provides for me in the shrine of the gods. I shall eat of bread and partake of righteousness [*ma'at*]."

Initiate eats from the bread and drinks from the milk or wine.

4. Consecration

Using their pinkie finger, the Officiant anoints the Initiate's forehead with oil.

Officiant: "Hail to You, oh (Initiate's patron deities), in all Your names and all Your places! Place Your consecration upon (Initiate) . May You make it beneficial to (Initiate) , and may You protect (Initiate) from all evil."

If conferring a degree or rank: Officiant places the vestment or other insignia, if used, upon the Initiate. Variation of above address: "... May You grant this pure vestment [or, 'pure office of ______'] upon (Initiate) ."

5. Address to the Gods, Group Members

Initiate faces the gods on the altar first.

Say: "Hail to You, oh _______, in all Your names and all Your places! Receive me and place Your arms over me, for I am Your follower [*shemsu*] upon this earth. May I be beneficial to You and to humankind, as You are beneficial to me."

Initiate faces the group. The group responds:

Group: "Welcome in peace, _________, welcome in peace! A place has been made for you, and we open our arms toward you."

Group shakes hands and greets the newly initiated member(s).

6. Closing

New member(s) drink the water from the offerings. Officiant rings the sistrum (or other instrument), if using one, to signal the end of the rite.

Group: "*In-un-ma'a.*" [Truly it is]

Historical Priests' Roles

Kemetic Reconstructionist groups in particular look toward ancient priesthoods when modeling their own systems of clergy. Some adaptations inevitably have to be made, as the ancient priests functioned in a different societal system than our own. But for those ready to map out their own Kemetic tradition and priesthood, the following background on ancient priests can serve as an informative reference.

Wa'b - Literally, a "pure one". This was the most basic level of priest. They assisted with maintaining the temple and performing ceremonies. They handled ritual objects, which required a state of purity, but they did not enter the inner sanctuary. To maintain their purity they bathed two to four times a day. Female *wa'b* priests, or *wa'bet*, have been documented but were less common.

Hem /Hemet Notjer, Hem /Hemet Ka - Meaning "Servant of the God" and "Servant of the *Ka*" respectively, these priests were of a higher rank than *wa'b* priests, though *hem notjer* priests held higher rank than *hem ka* priests. They saw to the needs of the icon statues, made offerings and performed rituals. *Ka*-servant priests performed offering rites for the deceased; in the Old Kingdom it was common for noblemen to establish endowments from their estates to support *ka*-priests who would perform their offering rites in the absence of living relatives. Female 'servants of the god', or *hemet notjer*, occurred more frequently in the Old Kingdom. Usually they served goddesses, though a granddaughter of Khufu officiated as the chief priestess of Djehuty (Thoth).

Khery-Habet - Usually rendered as 'lector priest', their title means the "One Carrying the Lector Book" (or "festival book"). *Khery-habet* (or *hery hab*) priests recited from scrolls of rituals and magic and presided over oracles and divination. In early times, it was a position generally reserved for royal family members and high nobility. Lector priests were the ones most closely associated with magic (*heka*). In the tales attributed to the reign of Khufu in Papyrus Westcar, the magicians who performed wonders were all *khery hab* priests.

Hery Sesheta - The Master of Secrets, or "One Over the Secrets", or "Overseer of the Mysteries", the *hery sesheta* was another specialized level of priesthood who presided over embalming and wore masks of Anubis, god of embalming who also bore the title "He Who is Over the Secrets".

Sem (or *Setem*) - Known for their leopard-skin mantles and frequently pictured wearing a braided sidelock, *sem* priests acted in funerary rites as the deceased's heir. They played a key role in Opening of the Mouth rites, not only for the dead but also for consecrating statues. They also took part in daily rituals and festival processions, such as the Haker procession during the feast of Osiris. Dialogue given for the *sem* priest in versions of the Opening of the Mouth suggest a trance-like state may have at one time been part of the rite. *Sem* was apparently a prestigious position, and each temple seems to have had a resident *sem* priest. Older translations give the title as *setem*, but more recently it has been rendered as *sem*.

Imi-er Hemu Notjer - "One Who is Over the Servants of the God", this was the chief priest or overseer of priests. Their primary difference from the *hem notjer* priests was rank.

It-Notjer - Literally "Father of the God", in the Middle Kingdom this was apparently a title of high rank and favor given by the king to certain officials who served as priests. Usually it was a special commission of cultic duties, though some scholars have also considered it synonymous with *Hem Notjer.* In the Old Kingdom, relatives of the king held the title of *It-Notjer.* This practice may have been revived by Amunhotep III, whose father-in-law Yuya held the title; it was also one title of Akhenaton's vizier (and possible father-in-law) Aye. In fact, Aye's full name was Aye It-notjer.

Hemet-Notjer en Amun - The God's Wife of Amun, called the "Divine Adoratrice of Amun" in older books, these were elite women of the Theban region. The title was bestowed upon Ahmose-Nefertari by her husband, King Ahmose, and it became the office of queens and princesses. The God's Wife of Amun led male priests to the temple lakes for purification, presided over consecration rites and burning images of enemies of the state. Both Hatshepsut and her daughter Neferura served as God's Wives of Amun. After them, the title all but disappeared until almost the end of the New Kingdom. Then, with the royal capital moved to the Delta, the God's Wives of Amun served as celibate *de facto* rulers of Thebes until the Persian occupation, when the position finally disappeared completely.

Shemayet, Heset - Feminine titles, these referred to singers or "chantresses" employed in the service of specific deities. The position was common for elite New Kingdom women, who were often the wives of priests serving in the same temple. Young girls could also serve as *shemayet*, often serving alongside their mothers and other female relatives.

Sesheshet,Sekhmyt - Typically women, these were sistrum-bearers. Both titles are named for the type of sistrum they used; *sekhmyt* sistra are the familiar type with a looped metal frame. *Sesheshet* sistra were made with a faience frame shaped like a shrine. Another title for sistrum bearers was *Ihyut*, referring to Ihy, the son of Hathor pictured as a naked child holding a sistrum.

Khener - A collective title, also spelled *hener*, this group of women has been interpreted as the king's 'harem' but may have actually been a musical troupe that acted as the performing entourage for the king or for deities.

Semdet – These were the non-ordained members of temple staff, such as bakers, butchers, weavers and custodians.

You probably won't need all of these positions filled within your own group. A likely progression might be from *wa'b* to *hem notjer* to perhaps *imi-er hem notjer* or *it-notjer* for senior clergy. Musically inclined souls could act as *shemay(et)* or *ihyut*. Just remember that without the *semdet* – the non-ordained members who participate in their own ways – the clergy are just a bunch of Egyptian Pagans standing around in white robes.

Hopefully this information will find you better equipped to help build your own Egyptian Pagan group. Share it with other potential members, and welcome their input as well. Most of all, good luck!

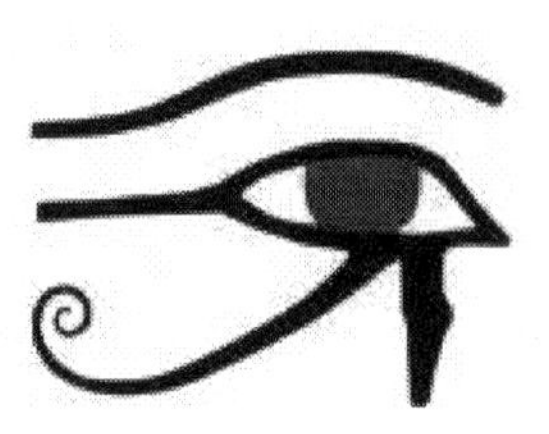

Conclusion

Years ago, when I first set about trying to learn ways to worship the Egyptian Gods who had a presence in my life, I had few resources. Not satisfied with the group traditions available at the time, I turned to my fledgling Egyptology library - and very quickly realized that my library needed to grow. And grow it did over time, from less than ten books then to nearly sixty today.

But not everyone has that luxury. Nor does everyone interested in Egyptian Paganism have the patience, nor the sleuth's eye for detail, needed to comb through pages upon pages of dissertations and scholarly articles in order to find details relevant for religious practice, then put them into a coherent whole. Learning about Egyptian history in order to appreciate it from purely an observer's standpoint is easy by comparison. Nearly everyone who walks into an Egyptian exhibit at a museum is awed by the scale of their stone monuments, the intricacy of their jewelry, the beauty of their painted art. But trying to understand how arcane-looking wands and ritual vessels were used, or appreciate the meaning behind temple reliefs, requires a unique combination of comprehension and imagination that most people outside of Paganism do not possess toward pre-Christian cultures. Egyptian Pagans certainly have the imagination and empathy to put themselves mentally in the sandals of the ancients, but because of the nature of the source material, they often lack the information necessary to start that process.

Addressing that gap in between information and implementation has been a major goal of both Following the Sun and this book. The rituals and hymns in the preceding chapters are meant as a springboard for anyone who feels yearning in their heart to honor the Gods and Goddesses who have made a difference in their lives. For those who want to know more, or try to gather information that they can use in a different way, all of the printed and downloaded sources I have used have been included. One of the greatest sources of frustration I found in my early days as an Egyptian Pagan was not knowing where established traditions got their information from - if it was all supposed to be based on historical material, where was that historical material? Why couldn't anyone read it? In some cases, the answer I found was that the source material - the translations of temple inscriptions, spells and papyrii - was simply too difficult for most people to obtain, often because it was out of print, prohibitively expensive, or published in another language.

The other realization I made in the course of researching Egyptian religion was that the source material is practically a Rorschach inkblot test. Two different people, or groups of people, can use the exact same translated ancient texts and derive totally different modern rituals from them. Commonalities will occur throughout, but the emphasis and intepretation will vary in the eyes of each modern Pagan reading the source texts.

It is for this reason that we *need* a variety of different rituals that are readily available to all Egyptian Pagans. No one daily ritual can be held as 'The' correct rite because no two will take shape out of the ancient templates in the same manner. Nor can the original texts of daily rites, such as the Daily Ritual of Amun-Ra at Karnak, be implemented exactly as they were during the eras that they were composed. Kemetic Reconstructionists in particular have tried valiantly, but a number of factors make complete re-enactment impossible: gaps in the text (*lacunae*), words whose translations remain uncertain, as well as architectural details that were incorporated into the original rituals. None of us have a whole temple complex at our disposal for rites of water purification, procession, or entry into an inner shrine room.

This is also why we need greater communication and acknowledgment between the sister sects of Kemetic Reconstructionism and Tameran Wicca. The primary difference between the two is simply to what degree ancient source materials are adapted; Kemetic Reconstructionists try to preserve the original framework of Egyptian liturgy and festival calendars as much as can be allowed, while Tameran Wiccans make use of the existing Wiccan framework and apply Egyptian material toward it. The former sect adapts minimally, the latter more liberally. Otherwise, however, both have the same goals in venerating the same deities. Quite a few Kemetic Reconstructionists got their start as Wiccans, and even as Kemetic Reconstructionists we still have to remain familiar enough with the basics of Wicca to be able to interact with Wiccans in the greater Neo-Pagan community. This is something we must be able to do if we are ever to gain the recognition we deserve as a growing Pagan movement. Mainstream Wiccans and Neo-Pagans will no longer be able to overlook Egyptian Pagans, of any variety, if they cannot avoid running into us online, at festivals or in book and alternative stores.

My hope is that Following the Sun and Circle of the Sun will inspire other people who pursue Egyptian Paganism, not only to try the rituals out for themselves but also to make their own adaptations and write their own. Hopefully some intrepid Kemetic or Tameran Wiccan will find even more ancient materials hidden away somewhere, combine it with something from a source or a ritual given here, and then share their new contribution far and wide. I hope to be able to read about a variety of Egyptian Pagan rituals going on at festivals, new groups taking shape, new books available online. I know all too well how frustrating and lonely it feels to be the only, "token" Egyptian Pagan in a Neo-Pagan community. If the hard work (and as it sometimes seems, spent brain cells!) I've put onto paper in these books helps one other Solitary Egyptian Pagan not feel so alone, and to feel that they have tools to deepen their own practice on their own terms, then these books will have accomplished their purpose.

To that end,

May Ra shine upon you,
May Up-waut open the paths for you, and
May Djehuty's wisdom be with you.

Udjai! Seneb-ti! ("Be well"!)

Appendix A

Titles of Selected Notjeru

To assist those interested in developing their own invocations to deities not covered elsewhere in this book, as well as provide more complete lists of titles for those deities who have been, this appendix includes titles for well-known Egyptian Gods and Goddesses (Notjeru). Some repetition occurs, as Notjeru are famous for swapping titles and characteristics. This list is also by no means exhaustive, but certainly provides a useful starting point.

Amun
Neb Waset - Lord of Thebes
Neb Khemnu - Lord of Eight-Town
Ka-Mut-ef - Bull of His Mother
Neb Pet - Lord of the Sky
Neb khau - Lord of Appearances
Nisut Notjeru - King of the Gods (as Amun-Ra)
Qai Shuty - Tall of Plumes
Neb Ipet-Resyt - Lord of the Southern Residence (during Opet)
En Khepy Nofer - Of the Beautiful Encounter (during Valley Feast)

Anubis (Anepu, Inepu)
Imi-ut - He in His Wrappings
Neb Ta-Djoser - Lord of the Sacred Land
Tepy Dju-ef - He Over His Mountain
Hery Sesheta - He Over the Secrets

Atum
Imy-Nun - He Who Is In Nun
Hotep - At Rest
Neheh - Eternal (Or Eternally Renewing)
Neb Neheh - Lord of Eternity (or Eternal Renewal)
Nedj-der-ef - Limitless One

Bast (Baset, Bastet)
Irit (en) Ra - Eye of Ra
Nebet Per-Baset - Lady (or Mistress) of Bubastis
Nebet Pet - Lady of the Sky
Notjerit a'ah - Greatest Goddess

Djehuty (Thoth)
Sesh Ma'a en Pesdjet - True Scribe of the Nine (Ennead)
Iker en saret - Excellent of Wisdom
Neb Ma'at - Lord of Ma'at
Neb Medu-Notjer - Lord of the Sacred Words
Neb Khemnu - Lord of Eight-Town
Notjer A'ah - Greatest God

Hathor
Nebet Yunit - Lady (or Mistress) of Denderah
Nebet mafket - Lady of Turquoise
Nebet Mehyt - Lady of the North Wind
Nebet Amentet - Lady of the West
Nebet nub - Lady of Gold
Sat Ra - Daughter of Ra
Irit (en) Ra - Eye of Ra
Nebet Pet - Lady of the Sky
Notjerit a'ah - Greatest Goddess

Horus
Sa Isut - Son of Isis
Nedj-Her-Itef -Defender of his Father
Notjer A'ah - Greatest God
Neb Pet - Lord of the Sky
As Elder Horus:
Ba Iabty - *Ba* (Soul) of the East
Akhety - He of the Horizons
Behdety - He of Behdet
Sab Shuty - He of Dappled Plumage

Isis (Iset, Aset)
Uret Hekau - Great of Magic
Mut Horu - Mother of Horus
Nebet Pi-lak - Mistress of Philae *
Notjerit A'ah - Greatest Goddess
Nebet Pet - Lady of the Sky

* Pi-lak is the native name of Philae, but this did not become a center of worship for Isis until the 30th Dynasty.

Min
Ka Mut-ef - Bull of His Mother
Qai Shuty - Tall of Plumes
Sa Osir - Son of Osiris
Mos-en Iset - Born of Isis
Notjer a'ah - Greatest God

Mut
Nebet Tawy - Mistress of the Two Lands
Nebet Isheru - Mistress of the Sacred Lake
Notjerit A'ah - Greatest Goddess
Nebet Pet - Lady of the Sky

Neith (Nit)
Up-Waut - Opener of the Ways
Nebet Sau - Mistress of Sais
Nebet Djedet - Mistress of Mendes
Nebet Tawy - Mistress of the Two Lands
Notjerit A'ah - Great Goddess

Nephthys
Nebet Notjeru - Mistress of the Gods
Nebet ankh - Mistress of Life
Notjerit a'ah - Greatest Goddess
Nebet pet - Mistress of the Sky

Nut (Nuit)
Mut Netjeru - Mother of the Gods
Kha Bauet - She of a Thousand Ba's
Notjerit A'ah - Greatest Goddess
Nebet Pet - Lady (Mistress) of the Sky

Osiris (Osir, Ausir)
Neb Abju - Lord of Abydos
Neb Djedu - Lord of Busiris
Khenti-Amentiu - Foremost of the Westerners
Un-Nefer - The Beatified (or Eternally Fresh)
Neb Neheh - Lord of Eternal Renewal
Neb Djet - Lord of Enduring Eternity

Ptah
Neb Ma'at - Lord of Ma'at
Sedjem Nehit - Hearer of Prayers
Nisut Tawy - King of the Two Lands
Neb Ineb-Hadj - Lord of White-Walls
Notjer A'ah - Greatest God
En Ta-sut Noferu - Of the Beautiful Place
Akh Pet em Hap-ef - Who Lifts the Sky With His Hand (during Makhir)

Ra
Neb Pesdjet - Lord of the Nine
Wa en Nun - Sole One of Nun
Khai hekenu - Appearing in Jubilation
Nub hekenu - Golden of Jubilation
Ka-Mut-ef - Bull of His Mother
Djoser-remen - Sweeping of Shoulder
Hor-Akhety - Horus of the Horizon
Notjer A'ah - Greatest God
Neb Pet - Lord of the Sky
Neb-er-Djer - Lord to the Limit

Sakhmet
Irit (en) Ra - Eye of Ra
Nebet Senedjet - Mistress of Fear
Khenti Per-Neser - Foremost of the House of Flame
Nebet Tawy - Mistress of the Two Lands
Notjerit A'ah - Greatest Goddess
Nebet Pet - Mistress of the Sky

Seth (Set, Sutekh, Setesh)
Neb Nubet - Lord of Gold-Town (Ombos)
Neb Deshret - Lord of the Desert
A'ah Pehty - Greatest of Strength
Sa Nut - Son of Nut

Sokar
Neb Rosetau - Lord of Rosetau
Heqa Iugaret - Ruler of the Silent Land
Neb kereret - Lord of the cavern
Neb Neheh - Lord of Eternal Renewal

Appendix B

Useful Egyptian Vocabulary

Amenty - west (direction)
but (*bwt*) - pronounced "boot"; taboo, abomination
Habu nu Pet - Festivals of Heaven
Habu Tep Teru - Festivals of the Seasons
heru suri - "day of drinking", day of celebration
hesmen - natron, to purify; euphemism for menstruation
Ia'by - left
Ia'bty - east (direction)
iri (doing):
... henu - receiving offerings; referring to gods
... hotep notjer - act of offering to the gods
... khut - 'doing things', referring to ritual practices
... ta mu - making 'water bread' (perhaps similar to our 'hot water cornbread'?)
iru, iru khut - things done
iun mu - 'bringing water'; libations for the gods
kari - shrine
khem - king's shrine, such as shrine of Amunhotep I in Deir el-Medina
kherep Serket - lit. "has power over Serket"; scorpion-charmer
net - 'regular procedure', ritual
Netjerty - adze used in Opening of the Mouth
pa suri a'ah - "this great drinking", festival
peh notjer - to "reach god", oracular petition of a god
qeni - sash worn by certain classes of priests
rdi en ta-hadj - "giving white bread", ex. *rdi en Ptah ta-hadj*, "giving Ptah white bread"
sa ronpet - amulet or protection of the year
sau en pa sehotep Sakhmet - amulets for the placation of Sakhmet
sau Serket - amulet-man of Serket, possibly related to the *kherep Serket*
saq notjer - a god's procession
seh notjer - "God's booth", referring to Anubis; embalming tent
Senut - Sixth-Day Feast, lunar observance related to Sound Eye of Horus; can also refer to national Dual Shrines of Upper and Lower

Egypt
suyt notjer - divine image; icon statue
sunu - doctor
uden - offering ritual
wa'h mu - water libations for the deceased - different from *iun mu*, not done for gods
wa'h hotep notjer - making offerings to gods

Egyptian Numbers:

1 - wa(yu)	10 - medj(u)
2 - senu	20 - djebaty (*reading uncertain*)
3 - khemt(u)	30 - mahba'
4 - fedu	40 - hem
5 - diu	50 - diyu
6 - shirshu	60 - shirshyu
7 - shefkh(u)	70 - shefkiyu
8 - khemnu	
9 - pesedj(u)	

Words for numbers are in some cases only tentatively translated. When counting, the Egyptians went from 'ten' to 'ten (and) one', 'ten (and) two', or *medj-wayu*, *medj-senu*, and so on, instead of new names such as we have for *eleven, twelve* and so on.

Appendix C

A Recipe for Kyphi

This recipe comes from Scott Cunningham's Complete Book of Incense, Oils and Brews. It contains a long and short form. Keep in mind that, while this particular recipe is quite faithful to our existing knowledge of kyphi ingredients, there are still certain plant and other ingredient names that remain untranslated from the original Egyptian. This represents one of our "best guesses" at true kyphi, or *kapet* in Egyptian.

Kyphi, Long Version:

4 parts frankincense oil
2 parts benzoin oil
2 parts gum mastic
2 parts myrrh
1 part cedar
1 part galangal (or ginger)
½ part calamus (or vetivert)
½ part cardamom
½ part cinnamon
½ part cassia
½ part juniper berries
½ part orris
½ part cypress
a few drops of lotus bouquet, given below
a few drops of wine
a few drops of honey
7 raisins

Mix the dry ingredients and seal in an airtight container for 2 weeks. Mix the oils, wine and raisins, blend with the dry ingredients, and let sit for two more weeks. Pulverize to powder consistency if desired.

Lotus bouquet – Combine rose, jasmine, white or light musk and ylan-ylang oils in equal parts.

Kyphi, Short Version:

3 parts frankincense
2 parts benzoin
2 parts myrrh
1 part juniper berries
½ part galangal
½ part cinnamon
½ part cedar
2 drops lotus bouquet
2 drops wine
2 drops honey
a few raisins

Mix ingredients as described above.

Books and Online References

Books:
Adler, Margot. Drawing Down the Moon: Witches, Druids, Goddess-Worshippers and Other Pagans in America. New York: Penguin Press, 2006.

Allen, James P. The Ancient Egyptian Pyramid Texts. Atlanta: Society of Biblical Literature, 2005.

Budge, E. A. Wallis. The Egyptian Book of the Dead. New York: Dover Publications, 1967.

------------------------. Legends of the Egyptian Gods: Hieroglyphic Texts and Translations. New York: Dover Publications, 1994.

Cerny, Jaroslav. Coptic Etymological Dictionary. New York: Cambridge University Press, 1976.

Collier, Mark, and Manley, Bill. How to Read Egyptian Hieroglyphs: A Step-By-Step Guide to Teach Yourself. Berkeley: University of California Press, 1998.

David, Rosalie. Religion and Magic in Ancient Egypt. New York: Penguin Books, 2002.

Fairman, H. W. The Triumph of Horus: An Ancient Egyptian Sacred Drama. London: B. T. Batsford Ltd., 1974.

Faulkner, Raymond O. Ancient Egyptian Book of the Dead. New York: Fall River Press, 2010.

----------------------------. The Ancient Egyptian Coffin Texts. Oxford: Aris and Phillips, 2007.

Frankfurter, David. Religion in Roman Egypt: Assimilation and Resistance. Princeton: Princeton University Press, 1998.

Gillam, Robyn. Performance and Drama in Ancient Egypt. London: Duckworth Egyptology, 2005.

Hawass, Zahi. Silent Images: Women in Pharaonic Egypt. Cairo: The American University in Cairo Press, 2008.

Hornung, Erik, trans. John Baines. Conceptions of God in Ancient Egypt: The One and the Many. Ithaca: Cornell University Press, 1996.

Lesko, Leonard H. et al. Pharaoh's Workers: The Villagers of Deir El Medina. Ithaca: Cornell University Press, 1994.

Lichtheim, Miriam. Ancient Egyptian Literature, vols. I-III. Berkeley: University of California Press, 1973, 1980, 2006.

Manniche, Lise. An Ancient Egyptian Herbal. London: British Museum Press, 2006.

Pinch, Geraldine. Magic in Ancient Egypt. Austin: University of Texas Press, 2006.

Teeter, Emily. Religion and Ritual in Ancient Egypt. New York: Cambridge University Press, 2011.

Youssef, Ahmad Abdel-Hamid. From Pharaoh's Lips: Ancient Egyptian Language in the Arabic of Today. Cairo: The American University in Cairo Press, 2003.

Online Sources:

Borghouts, J. F. "Ancient Egyptian Magical Texts." original publication 1978. Google Books. 18 January 2012.

Dennis, James Teackle. "The Burden of Isis: Being the Lamentations of Isis and Nephthys," pp. 52-53. Internet Archive. original publication 1918: digitally archived 2007. Microsoft. 26 October 2010. http://ia700304.us.archive.org/5/items/burdenofisisbein00nesarich/burdenofisisbein00nesarich.pdf

Dollinger, Andre'. "The Book of Victory Over Seth" (After Siegfried Schott, *Bücher und Sprüche gegen den Gott Seth*, Urkunden des ägyptischen Altertums, sechste Abteilung, Heft 1, 1929). An Introduction to the History and Culture of Ancient Egypt. 2005. Reshafim.org. 17 December 2009. http://www.reshafim.org.il/ad/egypt/texts/victory_over_seth.htm

Jauhiainen, Heidi. *Do Not Celebrate Without Your Neighbours: A Study of References to Feasts and Festivals in Non-Literary Documents from Ramesside Period Deir el-Medina*. Dissertation, Helsinki University Institute for Asian and African Studies. Helsinki: Doria, 2009. (ISBN 978-952-10-5723-6 (PDF)). 27 July 2010. http://www.doria.fi/bitstream/handle/10024/46975/donotcel.pdf?sequence=1

Maxon, Terry. "Anubis Stands Guard at D/FW Airport." Dallasnews.com. 2008. The Dallas Morning News. 20 January 2012 http://aviationblog.dallasnews.com/archives/2008/12/anubis-stands-guard-at-dfw-air.html

Muhlestein, Kerry. "Execration Ritual." UCLA Encyclopedia of Egyptology. 2008. UC Los Angeles. 21 October 2010 http://escholarship.org/uc/item/3f6268zf

Murnane, William J. "United With Eternity: A Concise Guide to the Monuments of Medinet Habu." Oriental Institute: Egyptian Civilization. 1980. Oriental Institute of the University of Chicago. 23 January 2012 http://oi.uchicago.edu/research/pubs/catalog/misc/united.html

Parker, Richard A. "The Calendars of Ancient Egypt." Oriental Institute: Egyptian Civilization. 1950. Oriental Institute of the University of Chicago. 4 November 2010 https://oi.uchicago.edu/research/pubs/catalog/saoc/saoc26.html

Poo, Mu-Chou. "Liquids In Temple Ritual." UCLA Encyclopedia of Egyptology. 2010. UC Los Angeles. 2 February 2011 http://escholarship.org/uc/item/7gh1n151

Quirke, Stephen, et al. "Festivals in Ancient Egypt." Digital Egypt for Universities. 2003. University College London. 30 December 2009 http://www.digitalegypt.ucl.ac.uk/ideology/festivals.html

----------------. "A late Middle Kingdom Account, listing festivals." Digital Egypt for Universities. 2003. University College London. 30 December 2009 http://www.digitalegypt.ucl.ac.uk/lahun/festivallistmk.html

-----------------. "Book of the Dead Chapter 125A." Digital Egypt for Universities. 2003. University College London. 22 November 2011 www.digitalegypt.ucl.ac.uk/literature/religious/bd125a.html

Ritner, Robert K. "The Mechanics of Ancient Egyptian Magical Practice." Oriental Institute: Egyptian Civilization. 2008. Oriental Institute of the University of Chicago. 22 October 2010 https://oi.uchicago.edu/research/pubs/catalog/saoc/saoc54.html

Teeter, Emily, and Johnson, Janet J. "The Life of Meresamun: A Temple Singer in Ancient Egypt." Oriental Institute: Egyptian Civilization. 2009. Oriental Institute of the University of Chicago. 15 October 2010 https://oi.uchicago.edu/research/pubs/catalog/oimp/oimp29.html

The full "Litany of Sekhmet" has since disappeared from its original source, but can be accessed from these two sites as of 25 January 2012:
<http://netjer.livejournal.com/2817.html>
<http://rasekhi.webs.com/praisetosekhmet.htm>

Online Resources for Egyptian Paganism:

There are literally thousands of pages devoted to almost every aspect of Egyptian Paganism imaginable. Attempting to cover them all would inevitably leave out something important. The sites below are meant to connect Web users to information and, ultimately, other Egyptian Pagans, and are not group-specific.

The Witch's Voice - While the members are predominantly mainstream Wiccan, The Witches' Voice is still an excellent place to network, learn about various traditions and find Egyptian Pagan groups. You can also advertise your own events or groups and submit articles. Online for fifteen years, it is certainly an established venue.
http://www.witchvox.com/

Kemetic How-to Guide - A bi-weekly (usually!) YouTube series covering basics of Egyptian Pagan practices, information about deities and historical background, and occasional controversies.
http://www.youtube.com/user/KemeticIndependent

Following the Sun forum - An open forum for Independent Egyptian Pagans to share ideas and learn from one another about various traditions of Tameran, Isian and Kemetic faith.
http://followingthesun.freeforums.org/

Virtual Temple of Tutankhamun - Has links, excerpts from ancient texts, photos of ritual altars and other information.
http://kemetic-independent.awardspace.us/

Index

A

B

C

D

E

G

Z